Delphinium Blossoms

Delphinium

edited by

c e c i l e   e n g e l

l o r i   a n n e   h a c k e l

j o s e p h   p a p a l e o

Blossoms

an anthology

D E L P H I N I U M   B O O K S

harrison, new york   encino, california

To our families

and the magnificent eight who helped

get us started

we dedicate this book:

L E E   K .   A B B O T T

B A R B A R A   L A Z E A R   A S C H E R

R U S S E L L   B A N K S

E . L .   D O C T O R O W

K L A U S   F U S S M A N N

V E R N O N   E .   J O R D A N , J R .

G R A C E   P A L E Y

P A U L   R U D O L P H

. . . and a special thanks to R.E.S.

Table of Contents

WE WISH TO THANK ALL OUR "FRIENDS OF DELPHINIUM" *for making our first book possible. We, a new publisher, are dedicated to giving the presence of publication to unknown writers, be it fiction or otherwise. A principal purpose of ours is to be able to recognize excellence in writing and try to bring it to public attention whether or not it is in vogue, whether or not it is accompanied by commercial success. Our only limitations will be our own aesthetic limitations, a universal onus.*

So here cometh

"Delphinium Blossoms"

To recognize excellence in writing

And bring it to the attention

Of the careful reader

Being a book of the heart

Wherein is an attempt to body forth

Ideas and ideals for the betterment

Of men, eke women

Who are preparing for life

By living . . . .

(In the manner of Elbert Hubbard,
          "White Hyacinths," 1907)

BE FREE, DIE YOUNG

BE FREE, DIE YOUNG

Lee K. Abbott

OWN HERE IN NEW MEXICO, DEATH ISN'T THE SPECIAL THING IT IS TO you outlanders. My wife, Darlene (who has a Master's Degree, is a reader and knows about such), says that the dark thing we're taught to dread is no more unusual to us and our deserts than wind which blows ardently or noise from an unexpected quarter. Out here, we die by wreck or in a tide of shed domestic bloods. We're a shooting people, we are, driven to temper by the common rages: envy, sloth in the one we adore, covetousness. Once, for example, five years ago, I was in the El Corral, a bar in which gloom predominates, and heard a woman addressed in the following fashion: "Honey, I like that flesh which rises to meet the meat which seeks it." He was a Rotarian named Krebs and did believe, evidently, in speech of the oracular kind. There was silence, followed by a commotion with the murder-filled head and he-man arms of a boyfriend and then, such as I see it, the usual end, meaning spilled fluids and the gray, loose flesh of that which, in another time and place, might say, "My-my, what a tender hold we have on life." Yes, I have seen these citizens of America shotgunned, clubbed with a two-by-four, clobbered by a Chevy pickup and dragged up into a twisted repose on a ditch bank, and so I do not bring to our story of struggle and demise much sentiment or the weep-stuff you find in picture shows.

Listen: I wasn't always the hard nut I am now. To be true, I was that youth you sometimes see in old drunks—mournful and misty-eyed and easily swept into melodrama. I had a dog once, Raleigh, that stumbled into my room one day, slack-lipped and not tidy as I knew him. "What's wrong with you, boy?" I said. His head cocked, I saw a yellow tooth or two, and then he pitched over like a log. Mother says I made these noises: "Aaarrrggghhh" and "Oooowwww" and would not accept for comfort any Bible-inspired language about mortals and the happy, fatted flocks that all animals gather into in the Protestant hereafter.

Which was pretty much my reaction—and why I'm telling you this—when, before I married her, Darlene's father, Dub Spedding, pointed a shiny lady's pistol at me, eyed me into silence and vowed to, if I ever bothered his child again, blast me over the raging waters of limbo and into hell itself.

This was 1968, you understand, a time of agitation I had sympathy with. To be honest, I was what my fifth-grade youngster Buddy calls a *hooper*, which is, as picture books define it, a middle-class creature with the hair and grave aspect of a bohemian; I had the slump of a revolutionary and went about, in these arid lands, as a teenage philosopher in Beatle boots. I said things like, "Be free, die young" and "Fact and fantasy are never twice the same." In the rock-'n'-roll band for which I was the drummer, Wet Places at Noon, I sang of wrath and tranquil islands in the outer worlds, then made flirtatious eye contact with the thirteen-year-old nymphets who worshipped us. I smoked red-dirt marijuana, ingested Black Beauties and sometimes, thrown into the underhalf of my character (that half of Vandals and Visigoths, in which we all share an interest), I broke into establishments like the Elks Club and did, to use the lingo we spoke in those days, co-opt the pinball machines.

I was in love, of course; and on this day I am talking about I appeared at Darlene's house in my usual costume of fringes and convict leathers. We were to shop, I believe, during which I could do something to express my outrage against the bourgeois principles of order and money.

"I can't," she said. "Daddy says I got to stay here. We're having company."

It was noon and I was standing so that I could see nothing but sunlight and dark shape. This was, as is said in story-books everywhere, foreshadowing.

"How long?" I said.

She told me to go home, she'd call. "He's real mad at you, Dwight. I think you'd better stay away for a while."

At home I snarled at the TV, then invented a song about pageantry and gore. I was profound in those days and liked to turn my vast valedictorian's intelligence upon what Mrs. Levisay used to call those existential questions—notions about identity and being which always made the FFA students and Vo-Ed folks sleepy as cats. In those times, I tell you, I was interested in what made this planet spin, why the upside seemed so often down and how the brain of Mr. Nixon worked. Now, I think of naught but comforts and how to preserve them.

By sundown, she hadn't called, so I tried her. There was, as you are right to expect, no answer.

"Okay," I said, "I'll nap."

I suspect now that my dreams were the vulgar male kind—wrought up with maidens and related froth; but, as I am now in a romantic habit of mind, let me believe that, at the so-called unconscious level, I knew something was wrong. My dreams, I therefore wish to believe, were turbulent as dark waters, heavy with peril, and omen-filled as are all moments before disaster.

It was the next day, Saturday, when I got up. No answer.

I told my daddy I was going over to Darlene's.

"The hell you are." He was a paving contractor, plus a County Commissioner, and had a direct way of speaking his piece. There was some work to do around here, he said. Specifically a willow tree to be ravaged and some compost to tote.

"Then I can go?"

He spit, looked into heaven. "We'll see."

That morning, well-baked by the sunshine we're famous for, I had these questions: What is going on? Where is that girl? We'd been going together for almost four years, and the assumption was that we'd be married one day. I was just in my settling-out period, I'd say, growing into the wise figure who could shoulder all those burdens parents hereabouts threaten their offspring with.

"Okay," Daddy said after noon, "you can go now. You be back at five. We're eating out, at the Popp's."

Lickety-split, I was there. Her place was deserted. I looked in the corral out back where Dub kept his horses, Bo and Skeeter. I rang the doorbell a thousand times. I sat by the pool for about an hour. I counted bricks. I even called the funeral home.

"This is Dwight Eugene Winger," I said, employing the polite voice my mother still loves so much. "And I'd like to speak with somebody from the Spedding family, please."

Dub's a mortician and, in keeping with the theme I am developing herein, well acquainted with death. He doesn't think much of it either—just sees us humans as bulk with several holes to plug. For him, death's the fact which feeds his family and makes him, of the six thousand folks here in Deming town, rich beyond want and able to laugh at this vale others find so tearful.

"Dwight Winger, is that really you?"

I was talking to George Dalrymple; in our high school, he was a dufus.

"Where are they, George? I got to speak to Darlene."

"I ain't supposed to tell," he said. "Dub says you're an old shithead and we're glad."

He was speaking for those other dipsticks who worked for Dub. They had their eyes on Darlene and saw me—in the context of the old story this is—as a Martian, clearly unfit for the darling who was the boss's daughter.

"I could beat the shit out of you," I said. "How 'bout I come down there and rip your heart out."

You could hear sputtering from that coward.

"There are three of us," he said. "Why don't you find a hole and crawl in it?"

All afternoon, I sat outside Darlene's place. I was in the grip of self-doubt, indeed. I had the sweats and such frets as arise when event exceeds expectation; I imagined, I now recall and feel no shame in admitting, that my thoughts were like downed power cables, snapping and whipping and spitting sparks. Later, I called everywhere—the house they had in the mountains that they went skiing on, Darlene's granny in Roswell, friends from her Theta Chi days, that meager marina at Elephant Butte where they took the boat sometimes. I was having, I realize, my moment: the crossroads of time and circumstance in which it is revealed to you, as truth is revealed to those bosomy heroines my momma is always reading about, just what you want and are henceforth meant to have in this world. I wanted Darlene; and I knew it just as I know now that I am thirty-six, a graduate of Texas A&M, and the sort of moral being who appreciates golf, drink, and the regular embrace of a wife.

After dinner at the Popp's (it was spaghetti and wholesome conversation), I got an answer at Darlene's. It was Marva, her sister, herself a knockout and dream-worthy.

"Slow down, Dwight. What're you talking about?"

Evidently, I was incoherent; it would be reported later that I sounded Arab or Etruscan and did use the language of madness and murder.

"You just tell me where she is," I said, "and I'll be gone."

"Daddy says we mustn't talk to you," she said. "He says you're a drug-smoking, cheating asshole."

There was some talk, she said, that I'd stolen an Oldsmobile and that I'd taken it, plus a sixteen-year-old blonde Wildcat cheerleader, into the mesa to do another thing the law would love to know about.

That wasn't me, I said. It was just fellows I played music with—Poot Taylor and fat Chuck Gribble.

"Daddy says you're taking money from a woman named Eve."

Then I felt it: "Darlene's with somebody, isn't she?"

"Daddy says you have no character at all, no ambition, no nothing. You're just using his little girl."

"Well, I'll be dipped," I said. I'd felt insight reach me like a fist in the ear. "It's that Frank Papen, right?"

"What Darlene needs, Daddy says, is a gentleman, not a punk who talks fast."

Frank Papen. He was one of those straight-shooting suitors who liked to hang around Dub, pretending to be interested in something more than his own daddy's bank. You can still see him nowadays, driving around in his Monte Carlo, wearing a flattop, and affecting the manner of one who is brisk in the business of mortgages and capital. His wife, I am told, is somewhat of a tragedy herself and keeps him otherwise busy looking up words like "solicitous" and the German for "despair."

"What would happen," I asked Marva, "if I came over there right now?"

Nothing, she said.

"Because they're off hiding someplace, right?"

I was smart, she said. Surely smart enough to see that my ways needed changing.

"Like what?" I said.

Like not be such a smarty-pants, she said. And maybe love America more.

"Marva Louise Spedding," I said, "you tell Darlene that I will be over at your place at ten o'clock tomorrow night. You tell her that I love her and that Frank Papen is to her what shit is to Shinola. You got that?"

"Make it later," she told me. "You're not supposed to know they're in Albuquerque."

That night, my band had a DeMolay dance to play and I attacked those drums as I had read that Batygh the Tartar had slain his enemies. The place was as you are probably picturing it: smoky as Dante's underworld, littered and full of din. We played my song, "Woman at Her Window," and made it speak for the many, like me, who were hungry but could not eat (which is metaphor and part of what I'm proud of). I was as apart from myself then as I am now from the boy who is the hero of this tale. I didn't drink, nor try a little of Poot's Mexican weed. Even Chuck Gribble's girlfriend could not tempt me.

She was wearing the outfit of an Egyptian and shimmied over to seduce me with her midriff.

"Mary Jane," I said, "I know someone that makes you look like the viper you are."

For dreams that night, I had none—not turmoil, not thrash, not mumbo-jumbo you get from Doctor Jung. I slept undisturbed, like a rock or a far-off fleecy cloud. Indeed, as I have since described it to Darlene, my sleep was that which does belong to, say, Clint Eastwood or those other righteous cowboys whose troubles are swiftly resolved by daring deed or single word.

In the morning, I was up early and went directly to my daddy.

"What needs doing?" I said. "I've been fooling around too long."

He looked around several times to see where my voice was coming from.

"You stay put, relax," I said, "I'll do the work today."

The way I figured it, even if they left now—Dub, Darlene, fawning Frank Papen, Dub's new wife Sylvia—it would take them nearly seven hours to get home. It was time, I believed, I could put to fine use by digging up Mother's flower beds or mowing the front yard. Plus, I sought to occupy my mind, turning its powers to such issues as which was weed, which not. Around noon, I had another idea.

"Ray Berger," I said, when I got him on the phone, "how much you charge for a haircut?"

It was Sunday, he said. I could come in on a weekday like everybody else.

I looked into my wallet. "I'll give you thirty-five dollars."

He spent a moment hemming, perhaps scratching his ear.

"I'll wash your car," I said, "pick up around your place, too."

By evening I had the hairdo you see everywhere in these times—lots of ear and neck, and impervious to breeze.

At home, I threw on a loud sportcoat Mother had spent a fortune on at the White House in El Paso. "Holy moly," I said. In the mirror was the person I hadn't been for five years. Had you seen him, you would have said that here walks a young man who has an upright God and keeps his face turned toward the lighter, higher airs goodness breathes in.

Then I waited.

As a man and a father and a taxpayer, I know many things now, for experience is a masterful teacher. I know, for example, the danger of impatience and why bullies are as they are. I know, furthermore, that we gringos are just one of many terrible, inward tribes. I know that TV corrupts and that there's more pleasure to be had in Babar and Charles Dickens than in the thousand laugh-filled hours after the TV news. I know we can be cross one minute, humble the next and, in the third, touched by such every-dayness as sunsets and certain music. But I do not know

1 1

now, as I did not then, how to wait.

"Ninety-nine bottles of beer on the wall," I sang, cheerlessly, "ninety-nine bottles of beer . . ."

Around ten the phone rang and I grabbed it up as if it were treasure. It was Marva.

"Darlene will be on the front lawn by the pool in exactly a half-hour," she said.

She had chosen to whisper, and I felt caught up in true mystery. This was an instant as rich as any from *Ivanhoe*.

"One day," I said, "when I am your brother-in-law, you will be able to ask me for anything."

Death. Say the word a dozen times and you'll see that it will mean as little to you as gibberish in French or what machines speak. Sung as we used to sing about what we thought was love in those days, it will no more touch you than trouble among South Pole penguins or a quarrel across town; it will seem to you now as it seemed to me then—a condition fetched up to disturb the small minds we celebrate.

This is how it was:

I beat Darlene to the meeting spot on the lawn and she approached like abracadabra made of chiffon and dew. She was wearing a nightie, and in the almost complete darkness she looked white as a ghost. She had the dreamy movements of one who has slept for two centuries. (On our honeymoon a year later, up in Hot Springs, she told me that Sylvia had given her Valium and something watery to ease her thoughts.)

"What's going on?" I said. "I heard you were with a peckerwood."

She had the fluttery presence of a matinee female, and in that moment I felt something dry and small break free inside me.

"I believe we're over, Dwight. They talked to me for two whole days, and what I know about you is scandalous."

She had a list, she told me, which included petty theft, disrespect and my supposed allegiance to chaos.

I said, "Look at me."

I drew myself up stiff as pride.

I said, "I am complex, Darlene." I believe I mentioned growth and described myself as but one point on the arc that was all youth. I mentioned, as well, that I had virtue— brought out now by trial and this tribulation; that, until this minute, I had been ignorant of my true needs. I loved her, I said. Were love electricity, then I had enough for a small country.

"Daddy doesn't care," she said, "he's coming out here to shoot you."

Dub Spedding had guns everywhere—in his night- stand, under the front seat of his Eldorado, in each of his funeral cars, plus a rack of exotic weaponry in his den. He had shot deer and duck, and once he'd winged a Juarez wetback who'd tried to bust in the back door.

So, in the cause-and-effect world we're looking at here, it was at this instant that Mr. Spedding came thumping out his front door, pistol in hand.

"Eeeeffff," I groaned. "Ooooowwwww."

You should have seen him in those days: three hundred pounds of hard meat, on top of which sat a mind that wondered of little more than ends and the means to them. "Robust" is a good word. As are "dark-browed" and "violent."

"Darlene," he roared, "get inside."

Holding her hand, I could smell myself: part English Leather, part ooze the fear glands sweat out.

"I told you, Dwight." Darlene was crying, her hands

flapping madly—to her hips, to her eyes, in the air like birds.

This was my thought, exactly: Dwight, this man is capable of eating you alive.

There was nothing for a second, then Darlene went flying from me as if snatched up by an angel.

I saw a light flash on in the Tipton house down the way and wished for an instant that I was near it.

"Daddy," she was saying, "I just hate you for this. I think he truly loves me."

Then she was stumbling backwards, spinning and holding herself where her own bullet might go.

"Boy," Dub Spedding said to me, "stop that damn shaking."

He came at me slowly. Lumbering. A thing familiar with disrepair and human havoc.

"Howdy, Mr. Spedding," I said. "How're you tonight?"

He fixed that gleaming silver pistol against my chin and I could feel an organ kicking inside. His face brought to mind the words *pitch* and *sulphur,* and he looked at me as others look at leaf rot or wastepaper. I was just an inconvenience he'd have to scrub off the porch one day.

"I know the sheriff," he began, "several folks in the FBI, even the Captain of the State Police. Your death will only be a remarkable accident to them."

We are one thing in this life, I was thinking. And sometimes we are another.

So then, because this was a long time ago and your hero was a fool, I said, "Mr. Spedding, don't say no more, just go ahead and do it."

The first dead person I ever saw was a ten-year-old boy who had tried to dig himself a cave in the side of a dirt culvert up where the Interstate is now. I was riding motorcycles with a couple of friends, Jimmy Bullard and John Risner, and we reached the scene as those ambulance people were pulling him out of the collapse and trying to revive him. It was a peaceful scene, what it was, blue heavens and vivifying sunlight and at the center of it—if I may be poetic—flesh which once had a name and a place in time. I remembered being struck by how composed that boy seemed. Though sallow-faced and blue at the lips, he seemed a charmed thing to me. He was not sex, which I knew a little of, nor the fame and riches we all wish for. He was not the world beyond, nor the future we boys sometimes talked about. He was, I know now, nothing—quiet, inert and eternal.

Which, I suppose, is what Dub Spedding saw in my eyes in this Wonderland I am writing about.

"Boy," he said, "what the hell are you thinking of?"

Darlene was elsewhere, sobbing and saying what a heartbreak she'd be to that father who'd killed her only lover.

He still had his tiny pistol at the point of my chin; you could tell he thought me as remarkable as a smart-talking Chinaman.

"I was thinking about the next world," I said. I mentioned that in it, as we were now, were me and him and her and it, his weapon.

You could see the air whoosh out of him then.

"Shit," he grumbled, dropping his arm and backing away. "Go home, Dwight. We'll talk about this tomorrow."

I speak of the foregoing now because of what happened this morning, and because I intend to leave you in a hopeful humor. Dub and I, you should realize, are great pals now. I am the perfect son-in-law and he, the perfect granddad, generous with money and time. And this morning we were out in the stable in the back, shoveling manure and, as he says often, chewing the fat. He's old now, mildly diabetic, and, as a retired person, he's given himself over to earnestness. He likes to speculate on the drift of the world and its current climate of decay. He likes to offer advice, particularly to the editors of *Newsweek* magazine. He sees them much as he did see me once upon a time—as brainless and inconceivable as talking carp.

In any case, what he said, while we drank Coors beer and shoveled, was this: "Dwight, how you think you're gonna die?"

It was early and you could hear the gay splash-noises of my children and Darlene in the pool in front of the house. This was our fifteenth wedding anniversary and we'd come over to frolic.

"Me," he was saying, "I'll probably go in a hunting accident or maybe a new wife will do me in." He was leaning on his shovel, in his eyes those lights you might find in, say, Old King Cole. "What about you?"

I knew of course. But didn't tell him.

What I didn't say was this: I am already dead. In a way, I died the night he put the gun to my head and showed me what a splatter I'd make on his pajamas; and the fact of it—like the facts of all these many and cheap deaths in the contemporary world—means as little to me now as does the former unhappy self I was.

"Dub," I said, "let's go have us a swim, okay?"

Whereupon I put down my spade and made for the front of the house to see that which I had and the place we are here for.

LEE K. ABBOTT

We asked Lee Abbott if he recalled aspects of the origins of his story "Be Free, Die Young," and he sent back this note: "I wish that I was able to remember even the slightest about 'Be Free, Die Young,' but, alas, all that remains is the awful recognition that I did far too little to cover up the clearly autobiographical with the normally big tarp that is my widespread imagination."

Abbott's highly original gallery of western Americans appears in four fiction collections: The Heart Never Fits Its Wanting *(North American Review Press);* Strangers in Paradise *(Harper & Row Perennial Library);* Love Is the Crooked Thing *(Algonquin Books of Chapel Hill), from which our selection comes; and the most recent,* Dreams of Distant Lives *(Putnam).*

He lives in Ohio, where he teaches at the state university in Columbus.

THE FORGIVENESS OF DAUGHTERS

THE FORGIVENESS OF DAUGHTERS

Barbara Lazear Ascher

HE'S BEEN LOOKING AT MARY CASSATT'S PAINTINGS OF MOTHERS AND children, and says, "You know, when I look at those children, I don't experience envy. I experience familiarity."

When I look at those same paintings, I experience yearning, a painful reach of the heart towards those moments when one could comfort. Fleeting moments, unlike Cassatt's which, captured in pigment, endure. Ours were interrupted by phone calls, dinner preparations, a social life. In Cassatt's paintings there are no bills to be paid, no meetings to attend. The dog is not howling to go out. Cassatt painted remembered moments of childhood such as my daughter describes, moments which rise to the top of memory's well and shimmer there above the more mundane and painful acts of family life. Childless, she painted from the memory of being a daughter, which is why my own daughter and I view her work from different perspectives. I look, and see not the comfort I gave, but the comfort I wish I had given.

I do not see myself as a source of reassurance and protection from the pains of the world. After all, she's now bigger than I. More outspoken. Strong in body and soul. When we stand, I have to look up in order to meet her eye-to-eye.

And I know my own psychic history. I know the times I let her down, times that weakened trust, drew a disappointed and hurt child away from her mother. The times she made me angry enough to scream in a rage that never enters the world of Cassatt's pictures. When she was two and defiant and when her defiance became physical in the form of a swift kick to the shins, and I, stunned, wailed to my husband, "I'm not sure I like her anymore."

I know of the two A.M. feeding when we were new to each other and my milk came so fast she would choke and throw up and cry, and I would try again, and fail—the milk squirting into her eyes, her nostrils, and finally down her throat, but with such force, she gasped for relief. We didn't have our rhythms yet. We were unfamiliar with our ability to comfort and be comforted. Both of us felt awash in the world. Alone, with our enemy, our beloved. One of those dark winter nights of pacing and feeding and burping and soothing, I stopped to look out over Manhattan for lit windows, for signs of others suffering alone in the night. Instead, I caught our own reflection and was shocked by my small size, by the fact that in my arms there was a human life, for which I was totally responsible. I thought, I'm not ready for this. I thought of the responsibility that would last a lifetime, and burst into tears.

I know all this and yet she sees me, through the eyes of

love, as a Cassatt mother. Through the heart of forgiveness, she speaks of my ability to make her feel that the world and she are all right. Children's forgiveness of their parents is a perfect forgiveness, forged out of love and lacking self-consciousness. Unlike adults, children's forgiveness comes from the generosity of their hearts, not from overbearing consciences shored up by community mores or church sermons. The most our consciences do is to form the words "I'm sorry," to demand that we put on a good show of it. But it is the rare adult who does not, when hurt, bear a grudge and wish ill upon the perpetrators. Children's forgiveness is another matter; it is natural, full-spirited and complete. So complete that it is accompanied by amnesia for the hurtful event.

One day recently, as my daughter and I strolled in Central Park reminiscing about her New York childhood and rainy days spent at double feature Fred Astaire movies in the Village, she said, "I'm so glad that I didn't have a working Mom." Her mind had taken a flying leap from the darkened movie theater to the present, skimming across the top of painful memories. She does not hear her ancient outcry, experience her loneliness, or sense of betrayal and abandonment. That blank in her memory is filled in by my own remembrance. Mother's memories are not as kind. I think of a night during my first year of law school when the family was gathered for dinner and her tears began to fill the carefully constructed well in the center of her mashed potatoes. "When I grow up," she choked, "I'm not going to betray my husband and daughter by going to law school."

I don't remind her. Not now. I would rather bask in this forgiveness, accept it as a balm. I hear the old refrains of the dangers of repression and am tempted, for a moment, to say,

"But you did have a working Mom." But I don't. I am silent as I am now as she tells me of the Cassatt paintings. As she tells me of love.

There is a place for nostalgia. It helps us to forgive. Her memories, incomplete and flawed, colored by wish as well as reality, make it possible for her to grant me absolution. I do not indulge in a confessional. I do not beg forgiveness. It's given without asking. Now, of course, the job is mine.

BARBARA LAZEAR ASCHER

" 'You'll never get rich and famous writing essays, you know,' an editor recently warned me. I know. But that's like telling a maiden in love with the peasant boy that love doesn't last long without wealth.

"I have no choice but to write essays. I think in essays. When a dilemma presents itself, when I don't know what I'm thinking, I sit down with the problem and the essay soon reveals to me what was on my mind. I suppose it is inevitable that I would get caught up in a rather nineteenth-century profession. My early training was in poetry, and that was followed by five years of rigorous legal training. Somehow the combination of flights of fancy with the discipline of reading law and writing legal briefs resulted in my writing in the essay form. It seems a fine marriage. Certainly one I'm pleased to be part of."

The word essay hardly conveys the form Barbara Ascher has created in two books, the recent The Habit of Loving and the earlier Playing After Dark; her writing creates the heightened personal quality found in fiction, and this intensity makes her insights lodge unforgettably in the reader's mind.

FÁTIMA

FÁTIMA

Brice Austin

ÁTIMA IS A WOULD-BE POETESS, AN UNHEARD-OF ASPIRATION; UNHEARD-of and worthless in the Rio de Janeiro favela.

"Fátima, fetch the water," her mother says every morning, "for the love of God get the water," she scolds.

Fátima gets up from her dreaming to go to the spigot. She carries two cans that once held olive oil. One in her arms and one on her head. Her mother scavenged them both from garbage. Fátima walks down the wet slum hillside for water, watching her feet, watching the mud push up between her toes, and that is a certain kind of poetry. "Black toes in Black earth," she writes later in her diary, "Black roots/ Nothing takes hold in Government land."

The women are at the spigot as usual, gossiping. The line is quite long.

"Iracema's pregnant!" they cackle.

"Nilton stabbed João!"

"Did you see Maria José? She ran from her house naked last night! Her husband had a board in his hand to beat her!"

The young men come down to the spigot, too, but they do not come to work. The young men never work. They come to flirt with the girls. Fátima is fifteen and she's pretty. They crowd around her, do the young men, their hair wild and uncombed as mad composers', their silky shirts open down to the navel, strutting like the cocks they bet on on Saturday nights.

"Eh, Fátima," they croon, "let's go behind the shack. Let's play mamãe e papai, let's play mamma and pappa."

The tasteless ones simply say, "Let's fornicate."

"O the thin men," she writes that evening in her diary, "O the thin men with their new moustaches/They whisper such lovely promessas/But is there a man in the dirty favela/ Who works, does not drink for a living?"

Later in the morning, she goes to the public school. Other children beat her and call her slum dweller. In Geography they learn where Brazil is. They learn where Rio de Janeiro is. Fátima would like to go one step further, but no one mentions favelas. She wonders, in this class, about the rest of the world. Why was she born in the one place she was? In her diary she writes: "Do others live like us elsewhere?"

After school, Fátima's mother calls her to help carry wood and scrap iron. It has been a good day. There will be food on the table. Fátima hauls three long boards. Her mother has two bags of scrap, mostly old cans. They trade them in for some money. The man who weighs the metal has no soul. He shortchanges them. Fátima's mother curses his firstborn. They go from there to the market. There is enough money for a kilo of beans. The man weighs out more than a kilo. He says he wants to lie with Fátima's mother. She says she can't afford to feed another child. She says she's too old. She takes the extra beans.

A woman with vegetables and children of her own is most kind to them. She has tomatoes and *xuxú* that are soon to go bad. She tells Fátima's mother to help herself to what she needs. Fátima's mother selects the best of them. They go home and cook dinner. They thank Jesus Christ. They thank Our Lady, the Compadecida. There are beans on the table. There is rice. There are bits of two kinds of vegetables mixed in with the beans. Food is a kind of poetry.

"Black are the beans," she writes in her diary, "Black are my feet/Black is the night/and the heart of the man who buys metal."

After dinner, Fátima lies down and tries hard to sleep. She has eaten quite well. It's not hunger that keeps her awake now. Tonight there is yelling outside, quite close by. It is the voice of Senhor Danelo. He is drunk. He threatens to kill his wife Iracema. She is pregnant. He says there's no food for another. She says that there might be if he stopped drinking pinga. He says they'll have to eat the baby to live. She shrieks and calls him the devil. He threatens to stab her, and the screaming begins. Fátima wonders if Senhor Danelo, who is old and rather grotesque, was ever one of the cocky young men. At last she drifts off to sleep.

"Fátima, fetch the water," her mother says every morning. "For the love of God get the water," she scolds. Fátima daydreams and pays her no mind. "Don't look so at the sky, for sky is just sky," says her mother. "Don't look so at the lagoon, the view is for rich Americans." Fátima gets up to go to the spigot. Again the line is quite long.

"Senhor Danelo!" is the whisper and cry among the women, "Senhor Danelo cut Iracema!"

"My God in heaven," says someone. "Is she dead?"

"Oh no, he cut her arm only. I myself called the authorities."

"Did they come?"

"Woman, they only come here when they have to, and never to stay. The Devil himself avoids the favela."

"Since when? I see him every day. He comes here inside a bottle of pinga."

The thin men come again today, the boys. They buzz about her like bees. They call her a flower. Except for the rude ones, their words are like honey. The longer she refuses them, however, the more rude ones there are. Now they make obscene gestures. They pretend to reach for her breasts. They are all little Senhor Danelos, she thinks. She goes back up the hill with the water. She hopes she will see the one man she likes. He is older. Sometimes he sits on a tire in front of his shack. Sometimes he is there when she passes. He is from the Northeast. Rumor says he has the blood of the Lampeão. Lampeão is a northeastern folk hero. He robbed and murdered. The harpies at the spigot say he's insane. His name is Renaldo. Renaldo has never said a bad word to Fátima. He has never asked her to come lie with him. Once he helped her carry water back up the hill. He did not speak at all. She has loved him ever since. Fátima's mother turned pale as a white woman when she saw him.

"For God's sake, stay away from that madman," she warned.

Fátima ignores her advice.

She goes to the schoolhouse again. Today they talk about History. The teacher swells up with pride as she speaks of Cabral. At no time does anyone speak of favelas. Fátima wonders if they came from Portugal on the tall caravelas. Were there slums on those boats? At lunch there is talk of favelas. The other children call her a pig. They say she lives in a sty and eats garbage. They offer her the napkins from their lunches to eat. She is tempted to take them. Her mother sells paper. Brazil has a history, she decides. The favela does not. No more than the tapir in the jungle has one. The slum is, was, and will be. Women get pregnant. Men get drunk. Children go hungry.

After school she helps her mother with the many sacks of paper. It has been a good day. The man who weighs it is friendly. He gives Fátima's mother a lot of paper money. She asks him if it is not more than it should be. He says it is not. She is happy. She says it's exactly what she needs to pay rent. He smiles and gives Fátima a piece of hard candy. Fátima wonders if he lies with her mother.

At home, Fátima's mother heats up the beans. There is enough left to satisfy. For two nights in a row she has gone to bed full. Her mother thanks God and the Compadecida. Fátima sleeps. It is a quiet night in the favela. There are no more stabbings. There are no wife-beatings. At least there are none that she hears. Fátima dreams that she is a poetess. She dreams that she lives in Lisbon. Day breaks.

"Fátima, fetch the water," her mother scolds in the morning, "get the water, lazy girl." Fátima has stayed in bed because of the dream. She awakes clutching her pillow and thinking of Lisbon. She tries to go back to sleep to pursue it. It slips away like last night's feeling of fullness. She comes awake hungry and in the favela. "Get up and get the water!" her mother demands. "No water, no breakfast!"

She goes to the spigot. The line is quite long. It looks as though it may rain. On a clear day even the poor have something, she thinks. On a cloudy day they have nothing.

"Senhor Danelo is back," say the harpies. "How long until he beats Iracema again?"

"Nilton drank pinga and threatened someone else."

"Who was it this time? The Baiano?"

"No, no. It was the little Lampeão."

Fátima's ears perk up. They are talking about Renaldo.

"What happened? What happened?" chant the harpies, and for once they give voice to the thoughts in Fátima's head.

"The Little Lampeão," says the privileged woman who knows, "told him to come back when he was sober and say those same things again. Then he would kill him."

"And then? And then? E então?"

"Nilton attacked him. The pinga made him bold. He had a knife but his head was not clear. The little Lampeão broke his nose."

"Verdade? Verdade? The truth?"

"Verdade. Nilton spent the night outside, on the ground. He woke up this morning both sober and humbled."

"Ai, ai. Three cheers for Renaldo! He's not so bad."

"He's a madman!"

"Perhaps, but they say he drinks no pinga."

Fátima is proud, though she barely knows the man. Once he carried her water and that makes him a special friend. She feels as if it were her own brother who did the good deed. It was past time someone humbled that Nilton. She fills her cans and hurries back up the hill, hoping to see him. The young men intercept her.

"There is the poetess," they say, and pursue her, "Fátima, write a love song for me."

"Oh, Fátima, your breasts are a poem," they say.

"Come, let's make a baby," says a rude one.

They all fall away as she nears the shack where Renaldo lives. They have all heard the stories, and they are afraid. He has never killed anyone except in favela legend. That matters more than if he really had.

"Bom dia," says Fátima. "Good morning."

He is whittling wood. He needs bathing. He does not look up.

"You are a hero today in the favela," says Fátima. "They say you are the man who shut up that Nilton."

He grunts. She waits. He goes on with his whittling. At last she turns away, disappointed, to go home. "Well, ciao," she says and starts walking.

It has started to rain. She is depressed. The day seems to stretch out forever before her. Then, without a word, Renaldo is beside her. He takes the cans of water and walks along with her. The cans are like cups in his massive embrace. His hands are large and rough and a little bit clumsy. They seem laced onto his wrists like boxing gloves. Fátima had a dream once that those hands were on her breasts. She has never told anyone. She looks out over the lagoon as they walk. It is raining. The view that was dismal but moments ago is now lovely. She steals a glimpse of his face. There is a certain kind of poetry in it. It is like the sertão where he comes from. The sertão is dry, dusty land. It is almost a desert. It is a land that men love, hate, and leave. It is a land they always want to go back to. His eyes are dry-blue and clear, like the sky there; like the sertão sky men see different things in. For some it is cruel, for some it holds promise, for some it is merely indifferent. His ears are large and flat and short hairs protrude from them. They look like two cacti.

"Is it true you are related to the Lampeão?" she asks.

He says nothing.

"Do you live alone?" she says.

He says nothing.

"Thank you for helping me," she says.

He says nothing.

They near her shack and she stops to take back the water. It is best that her mother does not see Renaldo. "Thank you," she says.

He says nothing.

"Goodbye," murmurs Fátima.

"Come to my place this evening," he says. He walks back down the hillside. It is still raining. She watches him go. Her knees feel like wet paper. She does not know if she dares go or not. She knows that somehow she will.

"O Lampeãozinho," she writes in her diary, "O Lampeãozinho, my little Lampeão/Quiet and strong, deep as the land/There is a beginning now. Let it begin."

Breakfast is coffee. It fills her up, then leaves a larger hole. She goes to school hungry. In History they study the Aleijadinho. His name means "little cripple." He was a sculptor. He carved wooden statues of all the disciples. He hadn't the use of his hands. He tied hammer and chisel onto his wrists. His work is the work of a genius. His perseverance gives Fátima hope. Living in the favela is like being a cripple, she thinks. She renews her vows to become a poetess. She has only a crust of bread for her lunch. It is worse than having nothing. It seems her stomach has no bottom. Her hope has no bottom. The other children come and call her a warthog. They call her diseased. She thinks of Renaldo and nothing else matters.

After school she helps her mother sell scrap. It has been a bad day. They decide to go begging. They walk around the lagoon. They both chant a singsong: "Alms for the poor. Por favor. Don't let us go hungry."

The lagoon is quite pretty. There are boats from the yacht club, their colored sails racing. The water looks cool and inviting. The authorities have warned them neither to drink nor to swim there. There is a disease in the water that comes from a snail. They say that it tears out the liver. It is called the disease of Prometheus. The lagoon is much like the city, she thinks.

"Alms for the poor. Por favor. Don't let us go hungry."

A man in a suit stops to give them some money. Fátima has found that, to the beggar, there are three kinds of people. There are those who give money. There are those who look away and quicken their footsteps. There are those who torment. She met one of this last kind when she was but ten. The woman gave her a tin of dried milk. Fátima was happy. She could mix it in with her coffee. She took the gift home. They opened the tin the next morning. Inside were two rats, half-decomposed. Ever since, she's had a fear of opening cans. Today no one does anything worse than scream insults. They collect enough money for supper. They walk back up the hillside towards home.

Fátima worried needlessly about how to leave the house. She forgot that tonight is the night of São João. It's a festival evening. Fátima's mother has prepared a surprise. She has made green corn pudding. It is a tradition. Hunger backs away from the warm meal like a slum dog from fire. His yellow eyes are still there in the dark. Fátima tells her mother she must go to the festival. Her friends will be there. Fátima's mother says yes, she must go. A friend of hers is stopping by, too. Fátima wonders if it is the man who buys paper. The sun is on its way down.

Fátima walks down the hillside. The sky is pink in the west. Ahead is the shack of Renaldo. Her stomach feels as bent and twisted as the scrap metal her mother collects. Renaldo is not at his usual place in front of the shack. She knocks at his door. No one answers. Now it is her disappointment that is without bottom. Night falls. She hears, in the distance, the sound of children laughing. The festival has started. She dares not go home yet. The man will be there. She decides to go to the party. She is leaving when a hand suddenly touches her shoulder. It is Renaldo.

"I was afraid you had forgotten," she says.

He says nothing. His hand is still on her shoulder.

"It's a beautiful evening," she says.

He says nothing. His hand is still on her shoulder. They sit down on his doorstep and his arm now enfolds her. She feels that he holds her like one of the water cans. His huge clumsy hand rests on her stomach. She strokes the hand with her fingers.

"I wish I knew all about you," she says.

He says nothing.

"I could tell you about me," she offers.

He says nothing.

"Look, there go the first fire balloons."

The fire balloons are made out of newsprint. They have one tiny candle lodged in the bottom. The candle heats the air inside and the balloon then rises. The light from the candle glows through the newsprint. On the eve of São João, the sky is full of such contraptions. It is a tradition. The government has declared it illegal. The balloons tend to catch fire in the sky. They fall in the city and create many problems. On the eve of São João, the city is full of offenders.

"Let's build a balloon!" she says.

He says nothing. He brings her some papers. He watches as her dexterous fingers do the work. He brings her a candle.

"You know that this is a crime?" she says with a laugh.

He says nothing.

She puts the lit candle up into the belly of the balloon. The air warms and it begins its slow rise. She knows it may crash and burn anytime. It may fall in the favela and cause someone problems. But it is so pretty to watch on the rise! The ideal is when it goes so high it's no longer in sight. The ideal is to have it blend in with the stars. The ideal is never to know what happened to it. "It's a beautiful night," she says once again.

"Let's go inside," says Renaldo.

"Fátima, fetch the water," her mother says every morning. "For the love of God get the water," she scolds.

Fátima walks down the hillside with a spring in her step. She doesn't mind the long line at the spigot. For once the harpies have nothing to say. They seem to go silent just as she gets there. The thin men come around, but are careful to avoid her. There is another young girl upon whom they focus. Fátima hears a rude one say to the girl, "Let's fornicate."

She does not lament that they leave her alone. She knows it is because of Renaldo. She knows they fear the wrath of the little Lampeão. It's as if she were branded. She feels proud, nonetheless, of the respect her lover commands. She knows that the women have been talking behind her back. There are no secrets inside the favela. She fills up her cans and goes back up the hillside. She looks for Renaldo as she passes his shack. He is nowhere in sight. She goes back to her own place. Her mother is waiting. She is pacing and stamping her foot. She looks like an enraged black bull.

"Is it true what I'm hearing?" she shrieks. Fátima puts down the two cans of water.

"What is it you hear?" she replies.

"That you sleep with the little Lampeão! Is it true?" Her eyes bulge out from her head in such anger. Her body shakes as one possessed in the rite of *candomblé*. Candomblé is also voodoo.

"Yes, it's true," she says.

Fátima's mother slumps with her head in her hands. She was ready to beat her daughter for lying. She was not ready for her to take the responsibility. She realizes now she cannot punish her daughter. There is no way to do it and not lose her.

"Ai, querida, querida," she mutters instead, "ai, darling, darling," she says. She shakes her stooped hand. Fátima wonders what it is that her mother wants to tell her. It doesn't matter really. She and Renaldo soon will be married. She moves out of the house that very same week.

Now no one tells her to go fetch the water. She does it of her own accord. The task seems much easier. She is living with Renaldo. He does not have a job. He makes his money by stealing. He does, after all, have the blood of Lampeão. She fears for his life on those nights he is gone. She begs him to stop. She tells him she will bring in money. She begins to collect paper like her mother. She begins to collect metal and boards. She must range far from home. She does not want to infringe on her mother's territory. She makes just enough to get by. Renaldo gives up the life of a bandit. He sits outside and whittles while she goes to work. She finds out a baby is coming. She tells her mother. Fátima's mother goes pale in the face when she hears.

"How will you feed it?" she says.

Fátima's mother changes her tune when the baby is born. She has a soft place in her heart for an infant. Now it is Fátima's turn to be concerned. For a month she cannot go to work. The little Lampeão makes a new appearance. Fátima begs him to give up the robbing. She goes back to work before she is ready. She aches each time she stoops for scraps of paper. It is worth it to have Renaldo give up his career. It is worth it when she is holding her daughter. The baby's existence is a certain kind of poetry.

"O tiny Mariana," she writes in her diary, "O tiny Mariana/Black child of Black earth/Black mud of my mixing/with the blood of Lampeão."

Renaldo has given up the life of a bandit. He sits in front of the shack and he whittles. He spends all his days there. Most of the men of the favela do nothing. Some of them visit Renaldo. They enjoy the stories of his days as a thief. He begins to drink pinga. When drunk, Renaldo is a madman. The pinga brings to the surface the blood of Lampeão. Fátima fears that one day he may kill her. She fears he may kill their young daughter. She demands that he give up the pinga. He begins to call her a shrew.

Now no one tells her to go fetch the water. She knows that she must. Each day now the hill becomes steeper. The line at the spigot seems longer. Renaldo's name is bandied about there like a bright, feathered peteca. Peteca is like badminton played with the hands. The filled cans of water are like stones in her arms. It is quite some time since she has written any poetry. The baby and husband are two crippled hands. It is all she can do to keep up with her work. It is different at night, in her dreams. Her life there hasn't changed. Sometimes she still finds herself in the cafes of Lisbon. She is always a poet. On mornings after those dreams she does not want to rise. Her eyelids feel as heavy as the two cans of water. But Renaldo is drunk and the baby is screaming. She rises. Hunger gnaws at her stomach. It seems there are a set of teeth in her belly. She feels pregnant with some strange child. The thing inside is sucking her life away. She thinks of her life as the colored shapes she saw once in an eyeglass. She turned the wheel and they collapsed in on themselves. She goes to the spigot for water.

That evening she is alone in the shack. Renaldo has left with his friends. They each had a bottle of pinga. The child is asleep. She sits alone in the shack. There is a candle that flickers in the breeze in the darkness. Her own life is as close to being extinguished. She has a knife. She runs her fingers back and forth across the blade. The blade is black with dust and disuse. The point is still sharp. She tests it by pricking a finger. A bulb of red forms on her thumb like a berry. She means to kill herself. The thought of her death is a certain kind of poetry.

She puts the knife point to her distended belly. The tip of it burns against her skin as she pushes. It bleeds some and the pain of her hunger moves outside. She thinks that when there's a hole there, the ache all will come out. She pushes hard and the pain comes together. Her brain fills with air. She feels light as a cloud. She is above the favela and flying. Below is a city of lights. Her vision is blurred and they seem to be candles. The dark city looks like the sky on the eve of São João. She feels so at peace.

She opens her eyes and her limbs will not move. Somewhere Mariana is crying. The sunlight comes in through the window. The candle has burned itself out. She still cannot move. The baby is crying. The sunlight comes in through the window. She thinks she should get up and go get the water.

BRICE AUSTIN

When we asked Brice Austin about the origins of his story "Fátima," he said, "At one time in my life, for nine months, I lived across the Rodrigo de Freitas lagoon from a Rio de Janeiro favela. The memories I have of that experience formed the basis for the story, though many of the specific details of the daily life were drawn from an unusual book I ran across, Quarto de Despejo *(translated into English as* Child of the Dark*), a diary of slum life in São Paulo written by Maria Carolinia de Jesus."*

Austin is now living in Laramie, Wyoming. Some of his stories have been published in literary magazines; last year he was awarded a Henfield Foundation/ Transatlantic Award fiction grant.

SLUMMING AT
THE BISTRO GARDEN

SLUMMING AT
THE BISTRO GARDEN

Eve Babitz

I T SEEMS LIKE THE ONLY PEOPLE WHO DON'T DYE THEIR HAIR THESE days are recently released captives. Of course, hostages are supposed to look tormented or, at least, like they haven't been to the hairdresser in quite some time, but everyone else on TV from the president on down seems able to stop at anything. This mentality, alas, is really bad in L.A. where the light is so pitiless, it's like being on TV all the time.

If you want to see all this striving against the ravages of being human in state-of-the-art proportions, go to the Bistro Garden on any Saturday afternoon, for it is there that the end products of all those magazine ads for face-lifts, body lifts, skin peels, fat suctioning, teeth bonds and collagen flourish in the gracious noonday shade.

It would almost look corrupt, except to be corrupt you have to have once *not* been and nobody in this place was ever that.

(Except the busboys, maybe.)

Perhaps I'm being too personal about all this exterior flaunting of wealth—those watches, that jewelry, those clothes from Rodeo Drive to wear shopping for clothes on Rodeo Drive. But if you're not used to this stuff, it's truly a scare to see women with Ann Blyth–young faces on bodies that, if you brush against them, don't spring back.

Anyway, it's gotten me down lately because what everyone says nowadays is true—all people talk about or *do* anymore is money. And it's not just my friend Warren, who married for money and now never reads a book or laughs or helps anyone but only tells you how much things cost and who spent his Engagement Celebration sequestered in the Bistro Garden so his ex-girlfriend wouldn't find out until it was too late.

I kept telling her he was always like that. I told her, "Deep down, he's really shallow."

"Deep down," she laughed, "we're *all* a little shallow."

"But he's not *kidding*," I insisted. And he wasn't. Deep down he was *seriously* shallow.

And when he returned from his honeymoon (the woman he married was 12 years his senior and took along her Yorkies, so you can imagine), he left a message on the ex-girlfriend's machine saying in a strangled gasp, "I still love you."

"Does this mean we can look forward to a divorce, Warren?" I asked when I saw him a week later, looking like he woke up screaming. But he just said, "No, no, no, no, I'm getting used to her."

"Oh," I said.

What has nearly happened to him is the exact replica of what happens to those 23-year-old manicurists who marry 55-year-old TV stars—those bouncy youthful brunettes who become frozen coral-colored women with chipless beige nail polish and take on all the outer trappings of women their husband's age who frequent the Bistro Garden. One woman I met there that day gave me the actual willies when she spoke; she was so listless and shaky.

"Who is that poor lady?" I asked my friend, Monica, the baby-shower honoree.

"What poor lady?" she asked, "Oh, Celia? What do you mean poor? She's rich. Very very rich. *Rich* rich."

"But she's so old!" I cried.

"She's not old, she's 34."

"Younger than me? She moves like Gloria Swanson." I meant *Sunset Boulevard*.

"Oh, well," my friend squinted, observing her friend closely, "she's married to this man in his 80s. Maybe she's just polite."

"Oh," I said, but I was glad I wasn't seated next to Celia because what is there to say to someone younger than you who marries for money, except, "How do you like your money?"

Warren is becoming frozen, too. All the life's going out of him, and it might almost be okay if the life going out of him were channeling into his new bride's bloodstream and making her look well rested. But instead, she looks worse.

That day, on my way into the room where the shower was being catered, I caught a glimpse of Wanda, the woman Warren married, and it was like being squirted with ammonia, she looked so miserable. Of course, Warren was miserable too, sitting beside her, but he was too bent on not looking married to look quite so unhappy. He looked, as Monica pointed out, like he was wearing a For Sale sign. *Still.*

It was the "still" that made me laugh, since he had

always looked for sale to me—at least until he fell in love with Emily, the one he called the minute he got off the plane from his honeymoon. With Emily, Warren convinced lots of people that he actually didn't care about worldly booty and liked having fun instead. They spent a lot of time eating hot dogs on the French beach in Malibu, taking long drives downtown to hear mariachi bands and having dinners together with too much cream and butter on the pasta and pecan pie for dessert. (They both got fatter, but since they weren't at the Bistro where everyone is in fear for their lives about arteries, no one noticed.) He was much kinder then, and I almost forgot my first impression, that he was for sale.

I remember the day they met. It was raining in May at this May Day Solidarity beatnik party in West Hollywood with lots of Miles Davis and lots of people who were going to O.D. or knew someone who recently had. Except poor Warren, who was from Boston and looked like Prince Charming.

Warren was six-foot-three and whenever they needed someone who looked like a "tennis lay," he'd audition. In fact, he looked more like Robert Redford than poor little Robert Redford, who's only about five-foot-ten in person at best. And if it weren't for the fact that even after years of acting classes, Warren was unable to do a bit on a soap without looking like an in-the-way bystander making the other actors nervous, he would have been a perfect Great Gatsby Lay star.

Warren had asked me to help him with his career, like all actors will do the minute they unbare their souls, so I was taking him slumming, hoping that character would rub off by osmosis. Besides which, I liked him because he read everything, could laugh in the most panic-stricken situations, and he paid for the smog test on my car—or loaned me the money in the most graceful way. He had noblesse oblige. I tried not to be in love with him, which was only possible because I was already heartbroken over someone else. So we were "just friends." It was fun having him at this party because he was so . . . *tall.*

Warren and I were talking to these two writers from New York who were exercising their brilliance over how stupid L.A. was, when suddenly the door opened and I saw Emily appear, closing a red umbrella, sprinkling raindrops on the cringing beatniks.

Emily was too much.

I mean, for one thing, her body. . . .

She was almost always too much in any situation and today was no exception. It took a moment just getting over how spectacular she looked. One bitchy lawyer girl always said, "Emily dresses like an incipient bag lady." But she was obviously jealous, because to me, Emily looked like a Lartigue photograph of one of those beauties from the French Riviera in the '20s. Today was a perfect example. She wore these huge baggy white sailor-y pants, this tiny clingy tight powder-blue T-shirt, these wedgies that made her six feet tall, and her hair tousled and wet from the rain. A lot of men had lewd conversations about Emily because they were so afraid of her.

"Emily!" our host Gary leered, because her nipples showed from the cold. "You came."

"But I can't stay," she said, looking around until she saw Warren, whom she turned away from, and then, unable to stop herself, looked back at, suddenly going all girlish and idiotic—in a cute way, of course—and she added, ". . . unless you made chili."

"Just for you," Gary said.

I just then remembered Warren telling me that his

mother was almost six feet tall, so maybe that's why he wasn't afraid of her. But the next thing I knew, Emily came up to us, ignoring him with a vengeance, and said, "Eve, my God, thank heavens you're here, can you give me a ride home, my car . . ."

(Boy, was she *not* looking at Warren.)

"You're Emily Bower, aren't you?" Warren asked politely.

"Yes, I . . ."

"I remember you, we met ten years ago in New York, you were with those Warhol people and I wanted to talk to you but I was too corny."

"Oh . . ." She looked at him, observed his Brooks Brothers posture—tried to hide the cardiac arrest his physical presence was doing to her and said, "But I like things that are too corny."

"Maybe I still am," he replied, and I could feel him rise to the occasion, fun-fun-fun was beginning to fill his heart and soul. And, for a moment, I realized that maybe Warren wasn't so shallow, if he could see the point of Emily.

"I read all your restaurant pieces," Warren said, trying not to lean right into her, though she was having trouble keeping a civilized distance herself. "They always make me laugh."

"Oh," she said, unable to think up anything brilliant—or more brilliant than—"Thanks."

"Can I get you . . .?" By this time, Warren seemed to have melted into her wave length and they broke away from everyone else, wandering out of the house—even though it was still drizzling—and for the next hour or so, every time I looked outside, there were Emily and Warren standing under this Jean Cocteau-y sad-looking rose arbor, looking into each other's eyes, talking. Emily, who always looked interesting at least, today looked like Dominique Sanda from *The Garden of the Finzi-Continis*. They both looked out of that movie, so far away and long ago.

So their romance began, and it broke into full swing in June when we all went windsurfing in Malibu every Sunday—or at least they did. I sat on the beach reading Italian *Vogue*, getting over my broken heart in the midst of their overflowing generosity. By July, I was able to plow right into another doomed flirtation with one of those French guys in Malibu, but this time I had the feeling that nothing could go really wrong again—or at least not that summer.

They used to go for walks at sunset and scare the movie stars—they were so much more radiant.

Warren actually started getting acting jobs. At first they were just bit parts, but by September he got a week's work on a sitcom, and Emily and I helped him learn his lines as I watched her infuse him with pride or charm or whatever it is you need if you're an actor and can't act and are getting by on star quality, instead.

And people who had always thought he was a terrible phony suddenly saw that he was sensitive and kind—which, when a guy is six-foot-three and arrogant, is a nice change.

And Emily, who people had always thought was crazier than a loon, suddenly seemed merely merrily eccentric—a view Warren was positive was true. Emily's magazine pieces became wise and cosmic, and *Vogue* asked her to do a big piece on all the restaurants in L.A. and become their West Coast correspondent.

The whole thing was turning out so great, and I was taking credit for it hand over fist. In the palm of those sunshine days, in a land where winter never raises ugly questions about survival and canning vegetables, fun was all the truth we needed.

"You are the two most beautiful people in all of Malibu," I would say as we drove home from the beach, stopping somewhere new each time for dinner, all tan and blond and too-L.A. for words.

"Where's the Noxzema?" Warren would ask in a panic, unwilling to leave the car without rubbing a lot in, since he was positive it made tans last longer. Camphor filled our hearts, long ago and far away.

What Emily refers to as The Accident happened when Warren was invited to a cast party for one of those TV shows and there met this rolling-in-dough widow of the executive producer—the woman with the Yorkies, face-lifts, collagen and skin that had been peeled but not enough—Wanda Lacks.

Emily and Warren had a fight a couple of weeks after The Accident and didn't speak to each other for a few days, which must have been why she was so sad when she stopped by my place for dinner. It was their first fight in the whole of their romance and she had no idea how it happened.

That night got really really cold all of a sudden—too cold even for October. It was as though summer had ended overnight without so much as a kiss goodbye. So we sat around all bundled up watching TV, when there, on the 11 o'clock news, we saw this horrible publicity thing about this charity event at the Bistro G and there was Warren, Warren in this black tuxedo we didn't know he had, with . . . that *woman.*

"But she's so hideous, so horrible, so ghastly, so *old*," Emily moaned, although she and Warren were my age and really Wanda wasn't *that* old, she was just so patched together it made it worse than she was. If it had been Georgia O'Keeffe, it wouldn't have been so bad. But there was Wanda, coming in from the cold with this lynx cape and

Warren. Maybe she came across as so decrepit because *her* husband, the late one, had been so much her elder. Anyway, the whole thing looked like she got Warren to go with her earrings.

"You know," Emily said, "he didn't just go with her at the last minute. You don't go to things like that at the last minute; he was invited before. And he *knew* he was going. He picked a fight with me so it'd look like he just happened to have this tuxedo sitting around waiting to go to this . . . engraved-invitation event."

"Do you really . . . ?" I doubted at first.

But I could see her point. These people had taken weeks getting ready to be dressed up enough; those charity things take months getting organized. Warren *knew*.

"Oh," Emily cried, "I'll never forgive him. *Ever*."

"Why would he do a thing like this?" I wondered, but from the cold winds blowing around my apartment outside, I knew. It was winter now and fun was a childish consideration. You had to come inside eventually, and it might as well be the Bistro Garden.

November came and whenever Emily called Warren, he said, "I'm busy."

It got colder and colder. It rained. Electricity and phones and cable TV, even regular TV and schools went out of commission. Cars slid into ravines. People were forced to go to movies or read books by candlelight. The Auto Club Emergency Road Repair Service phone number was busy, busy, busy.

Emily wept on my couch, her tears mingling with the wet rain on her hair, her jacket, her red umbrella.

"He's coming here for my Christmas party," I told her. "I invited him, he said he'd come."

"Ooooooo," she said. Then she thought for a moment,

"What'll I wear?"

She had lost 15 pounds over this—which I always envied in a person, someone who got a broken heart and *lost* weight instead of mainlining See's semisweet Bordeaux.

I always thought she was gorgeous, anyway, but now, so fragile and all, she looked like some kind of lily. She was pale from indoor life and moved much more sadly, and the joy Warren had mingled into her blood was drained into the past. Her friend, Marika Contompasis, gave her this incredible sweater, ecru with pale colors woven through it and little pieces of old ribbon, lace and fabric. Marika gave her a long pleated skirt, off-white, too. And Emily had these old white shoes, so when she got all dressed for the party, she looked just like a faded photograph of some Henry James croquet virgin.

When Warren arrived, wearing these horrible Rodeo Drive presents Wanda bought him, which were Too Loud, and he saw Emily, his face just fell and he began to tremble and suddenly, the two of them were mingled together, laughing like they had never stopped. But Warren looked at his watch and said, "I've got to go. I'm expected somewhere."

And he left.

What discipline.

I guess *that* is what they mean by "character" on the East Coast: leaving summer behind.

(As though it would never come again.)

And it turned out that he was on his way to his Engagement Party at the Bistro Garden and leaving that night for Bermuda, where he married Wanda on New Year's Eve.

"When I heard about it," Emily said, "I thought I was okay and I just went swimming at the Ambassador Hotel like I always do. But in the parking lot, in the parking lot, I just . . ."

And she began to cry again.

And then, two weeks later, we came in from going to see the new Laddie Dill art and she turned on her machine and we heard this croak, this voice of Warren in a strangled gasp saying, "I still love you."

"Is that . . . ?" I asked.

"Never mind," she said, and erased it. "It's probably a wrong number."

But I knew Warren's voice, even strangled, it was Warren—

"But it's . . ." Then I thought, So what, after all, unless he's getting a divorce. And he had told me he was getting "used to her," so . . .

So it's been like that for a few years now, this torment between Emily and Warren.

And I was there at my friend Monica's baby shower, in this decorated blue room (they knew it was going to be a boy and they'd already named it Alan—so much for yellow), sitting next to Marika, the sweater-maker, ignoring the Godiva chocolate favors we all got, when I looked up and there was Warren, staring at me across this roomful of pastel women all talking a mile a minute.

I excused myself and went out a side door, meeting Warren by the ladies room at the end of the bar, and there we were, for a moment, in silence.

"Hi," he said.

"So," I said. (I looked at his stupid expensive shoes, his stupid expensive pants, his ridiculous neon-blue Las Vegas silk shirt—Wanda's favorite color for him—this ridiculous silk handkerchief stuck in his stupid jacket pocket.)

"I heard you're doing great," he said. "How are you?"

"I'm *fine*!" I said forcefully. "How are *you*!?"

(He looked like a drunk Irish priest, *old*.)

For a moment I thought he was going to reply something eminently civilized and suitable for the Bistro Garden on a Saturday afternoon among all these stupid flowers. But instead, to the question, "How are you?" he just cracked. He began laughing so hard he had to lean against a wall.

I shook my head, grabbed a cocktail napkin to brush a tear off my face, blew my nose, and left him there limp against the doorway, laughing, with this horrible stupid new color on his hair and dyed eyelashes. If the scene had had any character to it at all, it could have been *Death in Venice*. But to be corrupt, you must once have been innocent—and I guess some people never were.

At least some were, though.

Emily is still in love with him and insists he couldn't have dyed his hair, that it's just a rinse.

"It'll grow back out," she says, determined to still think he's wonderful. And through her eyes, it might be true. She just seems to get younger and younger. Ever since she lost all that weight when they broke up, she has just stayed this Daisy Miller virgin, waiting for him to come home from the stupid winter madness, back to where the sun is forever warm and where no rains ever made a tall girl sad.

E V E   B A B I T Z

Ever since she gathered a loyal following after her first collection of short stories (dealing with sixties people) was published, Eve Babitz had been a witty and accurate recorder of Los Angeles "culture."

And now, ten years later, the Babitz eye is watching the eighties in the Bistro Garden, just as sharp and authentic as ever, noting the changes of the times in the people. We hope for another collection like her Slow Days, Fast Company.

In the late seventies Babitz published a novel, Sex and Rage, *which, like her short story collection, was published by Knopf. Eve is currently working on a new book, writes articles for magazines, and has her own column in* Smart *magazine.*

THE VISITOR

THE VISITOR

Russell Banks

I N LATE APRIL OF A
RECENT YEAR, I DROVE FROM MY HOME IN NEW
York City across New Jersey to deliver a lecture at East
Stroudsburg University, which is located in Pennsylvania at
the southern end of the Pocono Mountains, not far from the
Delaware Water Gap. I arrived a few hours earlier than my
hosts expected me, so that, once there, I was free to drive 35
miles further north to the small town of Tobyhanna, where
my mother and father lived with me and my brother and
sister for a single year, 1952, when I was 12, my brother 10
and my sister six.

For the five of us, the year we lived in Tobyhanna was
the most crucial year of our shared life. It defined us: we
were that family, we have remained that family. The following summer, my mother and father got divorced, and from
then on, although we were the same, everything else was
different. Not better, just different.

Looking back, I see that both my parents were careening out of control with rage, frustration, and fear. For years, my father had been plotting ways to leave my mother, whose dependency and hysteria had imprisoned him then, as later it would me. For her part, my mother had been just as busy trying to keep him from leaving, which only made him feel more trapped today than yesterday. He was 38; his life was skidding past. And he thought he was somehow better than she, a more important person in the overall scheme of things than she, and he acted accordingly. This made my mother wild.

My father was a plumber, and he had been hired by a New England contractor as superintendent of all the plumbing, heating, and air conditioning installation in an enormous army shipping and storage depot then being built in Tobyhanna. It was one of the first big postwar military bases commissioned by the Eisenhower administration. My father was the company's man sent down from Hartford to run its largest out-of-state job, an extraordinary position for a young journeyman pipefitter with no more than a high school education, a man whose biggest job up to then had been adding a wing to the Veterans' Hospital in Manchester, New Hampshire. But he was bright, and he worked hard, and he was very good-looking and lucky. People liked him, especially men, and women flirted with him.

He was a heavy drinker, though, starting it earlier every day. And with each additional long night's stay at the bar in Tobyhanna, he turned increasingly nasty and sometimes violent. The job he held was, in fact, way over his head, and he was terrified—not of being fired, but of being found out, and not so much by other people, as by himself.

I drove my car into Tobyhanna, a poor bedraggled batch of houses and garages and trailers strung along a winding two-lane road abandoned long ago for the Stroudsburg–Scranton highway, and saw at once the bar where my father used to spend his evenings after work and as much of his weekends as he could steal from the house in the woods where he had established his nervous wife and three children. It was a small, depressing impoverished town, despite the presence of the army depot—or perhaps because of it.

I drew my car up to the bar on the main street, shut off the motor, and went inside. It was dark, dirty, and damp, smelled of old beer, sweat, and pickled hard-boiled eggs, with a jukebox at the back, a U-shaped linoleum-covered bar that ran the length of the room, and several dim flickering neon beer signs in the window.

I ordered a beer from the middle-aged woman behind the bar, whose exact round dun-colored double—her twin, I thought, or surely her sister—sat on a stool on the other side of the bar. She sat next to a man with a tracheotomy who was talking to her in a harsh electronic moan.

A second man was perched on a stool a ways down from me—a scrawny fellow in his mid-fifties whose arms were covered with badly drawn tattoos. His head was wobbling on his neck above a bottle of beer, and he seemed not to notice when I sat down. The place had not changed a bit in the 34 years since I last entered it. The doubling image of the round woman behind the bar and the woman sitting by the man with the hole in his throat acted like a drug or a mathematical formula or a vision, instantly doubling the place itself with my memory of it, matching my arrival in Tobyhanna today with my memory of a Saturday in winter, when my father drove me and my younger brother into town with him—ostensibly to pick up a few groceries or some such errand.

It's no longer clear to me why we three males left the house and hearth for town that day, just as it was not clear to me why I decided to drive north from Stroudsburg, when I more easily and pleasantly could have strolled around the college campus for a few hours, killing time. There was a powerful need to go there, but no remembered reason.

I remember my father bringing my brother and me straight into the bar with him, and I remember his cronies—soldiers and construction workers—buying my brother and me Cokes and potato chips. They teased us and praised us for our manly cleverness, we were little men, while down along the bar my father leaned over a friend's shoulder and talked intently into his ear, then smiled at a fat woman (or so she looked to me) with bright red lipstick sitting next to him and patted her forearm affectionately and soon switched his attention completely over to her, leaving his male friend to drink alone for a while. I watched this take place.

The bartender waddled over to me, picked up my nearly empty bottle, and studied it and set it back down. "Want another?" I shook my head no.

She lit a cigarette, inhaled furiously, a large red-faced woman smoking like a steamship, and she studied my face the way she had examined my beer bottle. "You're not from around here," she stated.

"Last time I was in here was 34 years ago," I said.

She laughed, once, more a bark than a laugh. "It hasn't changed."

"Nope," I said. "It's the same." The man next to me at the bar, his head wobbling like a heavy flower on a stem, was alert, more or less, and watching me now.

"You ain't old enough to've been in here 34 years ago," he growled.

"I was only a kid then. With my father. My father brought me in here."

The man sat up straight and swept his arms around and then pointed at each of the four corners of the dingy room. "This place, it hasn't changed," he said. "Where are you from?"

"New York City."

"Hah!" he laughed. "This," he said, waving his arms again, indicating the three other people in the bar as if they were a place, "this is the way to live! You never lock your doors here. It's safe," he proclaimed. "Not like, not like your goddamned New York City."

I nodded in agreement, got off my stool, and made for the door. He called after me, "Hey buddy! You're welcome!" He grinned through loose red lips and broken teeth and started to cackle at his joke on me and then cough and finally wheeze and whoop, as I hurried out the front door to my car.

On our way home from the bar, me in front in the passenger's seat, my brother in back, my father had said, "Listen, boys, let's just say we spent the time at the depot. In the office. I should've gone over some drawings there anyhow, so we might as well say that's what we did, right?" He looked over at me intently. "Right?"

"Sure," I said. "I don't care."

I peered out the window at the gauze curtains of snow falling, the houses that occasionally flashed past, the dark shadows of trees and of the Poconos closing off the sky. I didn't care.

My brother didn't say anything, but my father never asked him to. I was the one he worried about; I was the one my mother would interrogate.

The house itself had not changed. Except for the coat of

blue-gray paint, it was still the same two-story farmhouse with the long shed attached at the rear and the weather-beaten, unpainted barn across from the circular drive. The two stone chimneys at the ends of the house were matched by the pair of huge maple trees next to the road. Hanging from one of the trees was a small wooden sign. Rettstadt's Restaurant, it said. *Serving Dinners Fri. to Sat., 5 PM to 9 PM.* I could not imagine who would drive all the way out from Tobyhanna—five miles through the woods on a narrow winding hilly road, passing barely a dozen other houses on the way, broken-down and half-finished bungalows and trailers set on cinderblocks among car chassis and old refrigerators and tires—for dinner at Rettstadt's. I looked at my watch, 4:45, and drew my car off the road, pulled into the driveway, and parked by the back porch, facing the door that, when we lived there, opened into the kitchen. By now, my limbs felt weak and awash with blood, and my heart was pounding furiously, as if I were at the entrance to a cave.

By the time my father and brother and I arrived home, the snow was coming down heavily, and my father told my mother that the snow had slowed him up, he had got stuck twice, and besides, he had to spend quite a while at the office at the depot working on some drawings for Monday. That was why we were so late getting home from town.

My mother looked at him wearily. It was the same old story, the same old challenge tossed down, the dare for her to take him on one more time: either believe the liar or enrage him by forcing him to tell the truth.

I know from photographs that my mother was a pretty woman—small, blond, precisely featured, with lively hazel eyes and a sensitive mouth. "Petite," she liked to say of herself. People said she looked like beautiful women—Claudette Colbert, Ann Blyth, Bette Davis—and she did.

Not like any one of them, but she belonged to that particular caste of beauty. I remember her that afternoon as standing before the stove, a ladle in hand, a steaming pot before her—but that, too, is a generic image, like her beauty. It was a Saturday afternoon, it was snowing.

My brother dodged around her and disappeared like a mouse through the living rooms toward the stairs and the unused bedroom on the second floor, a kind of attic in the back where we had set up our electric trains. My sister—I have no idea where she was, possibly in the kitchen, possibly with a friend for the afternoon: country children often visited each other on weekends; it made the driving back and forth easier for the parents. I hung around by the kitchen door, as if waiting for orders from one or the other of my parents. They were looking angrily at one another, however, and did not seem to know that I existed.

My mother said, "I know where you've been, I can smell it on you. I can smell her, too."

My father's face reddened, and he glowered down at her from his full height, which, because my mother was small and I was only 12 years old, seemed a considerable height, though he was never any taller than six feet, which turned out to be my height as well. He began to shout at her. It was at first a welling up and then an overflow of anger, wordless—or no words that I can recall—a kind of sustained roar, which she answered by letting loose with shrieks, cries, calls, wails—again, with no words that I can recall now and surely could not hear then, for the tone was all one needed in order to understand the sad rage this man and woman felt toward one another, like a pair of beasts caught side by side, each with a limb in the jaws of the same cruel trap.

What in 1952 had been the kitchen was now a restaurant dining room, the floor covered with bright green indoor-outdoor carpeting, the walls paneled over in imitation pine with five-and-dime framed pictures of a trout stream with a deer bending its head to drink, a barn and silo and amber waves of grain, a covered bridge with throngs of fall foliage behind it. I smelled food cooking, and I walked through the door that had once led to the woodshed behind the kitchen and discovered that it led now to a large open room filled with stainless steel counters, dishwashers, sinks, and stoves. I saw in the far corner of the room a small man in white pants and T-shirt scrubbing utensils in a sink. He saw me and waved, as if he'd been expecting me. He was in his late fifties, I guessed, square-faced, short, thick-bodied.

I said, "I'm not here to eat, don't worry."

He smiled and nodded. "We're not set up yet, anyhow. Too early friend."

"Yes, well, I'm not here to eat," I repeated. "I used to live here."

He squinted across the room at me. Then he pursed his lips and pronounced my last name. My very name.

"Yes!" I said, astonished. "That's right!" I did not know this man, I had never seen him before. I felt my father loom up beside me, huge and red and full of heat, and I looked automatically to my left, where I felt his presence most, and leaned away from him, then recovered and stood straight and regarded the small man in white below me. He put down the spoon he'd been scrubbing and took a step closer. He said my father's first name and his last. "The plumber. Right? The plumber?"

"Well, yes. My father. I'm not him, though. I'm his son." He examined my face for a few seconds, as if he did not believe me. He was looking at a gray-haired man in his late forties, a man nearly a decade older than my father had been in 1952. I was, however, more likely my father than my father's son.

I told him that my father had died five years ago.

He was sad to hear that and asked what he died of.

"Liver," I said. "He pretty much drank himself to death."

He nodded. "Yeah, well, those construction guys. They all hit the booze pretty hard. I ran the food concession for the job your dad was on, down there at the depot," he said. "I was a kid then, just out of the service. I knew your dad, what a guy he was! Memorable. He had what you call real personality, your dad." He wiped his hands with a towel and stuck one out to shake. "George Rettstadt," he said. "I bought this place a few years after your dad lived here. He rented it, right? Brought your mom and the kids out from someplace in New England for a while, right? C'mon and look around, if you want. I've made loads of changes, as you can see," he said, waving his arms at the four corners of the room, just like the drunk at the bar.

I agreed. There had been a lot of changes. But even so, it was the same house, and it smelled the same to me, the light fell at familiar angles through the maple trees and tall narrow windows, rooms opened into rooms where they always had. Rettstadt had turned woodshed into kitchen and kitchen into dining room, he had covered walls and floors, and he had lowered ceilings, hung brass lamps and tacky pictures. He had altered the whole function of the house, though he still lived in it, he assured me, upstairs. The living room was now a large second dining room that was for private parties, which he said was most of his business. "You know, Lions Club, Boy Scouts, stuff like that. Reunions, weddings, like that."

Rettstadt walked ahead of me, pointing out the

changes, while I saw only the house that lay hidden beneath this one, the white house under the blue one, the drab decaying farmhouse in the woods where a young man had stuck his unhappy wife and bewildered children while he drove into town to work every day and to drink every night and tried to invent a man he could never become. On that snowy Saturday long ago, while my mother shrieked at my father and he bellowed back, barking like an angry dog at her small spitting face, I finally darted past them and fled the kitchen for the bedroom upstairs that I shared with my brother. It was a corner room with a pair of long windows on one side and our twin beds on the other. I remember lying on my bed, the one nearer the windows, reading a comic book, probably, with my wet feet on the clean bedspread, my arm crooked back to support my head, when suddenly the door flew open, and my mother was hovering over me like a great bird, clutching my shirt and yanking me up beside her on the bed.

"Tell me!" she cried. "Tell me where you went! Don't you lie to me, too!" She raised her hand and held it, palm out, a few inches from my face, as if she wanted me to read it, and she said, "Don't you lie to me, too, or I swear, I'll go crazy. Tell me where you went all afternoon. I know he took you to the bar in town. He did, didn't he? He didn't get stuck in the snow, and he didn't go to the depot. He just went to the bar. And there was a woman there, I know it. Tell me the truth."

I did not protest, I did not hesitate. I nodded my head up and down, and said, "We went to the bar in town. Nowhere else."

She smiled, wiped the tears from her cheeks and stood. "Good boy," she said. "Good boy." She turned and left the room. I lay back down trembling, and in a few seconds the buzz of the electric trains from the attic room in back replaced the buzz in my head, and I believe I fell asleep.

When George Rettstadt asked me if I wanted to see how he'd changed the rooms upstairs, where he said he had fixed up a large apartment for himself and his wife, I felt my chest tighten. "No," I said very quickly, as if he had invited me to look steadily at a gruesome object. "No, that's okay, I'm in kind of a hurry, anyhow," I said, easing toward the door. "I wanted to walk around the yard a minute. I wanted to see where my brother and sister and I used to play. You know."

Rettstadt said, "Sure, take all the time you want. Look at whatever you want to look at, everything's unlocked. We never lock our doors out here, you know." He opened the door, we shook hands, and I stepped out, breathing rapidly.

I did poke into the barn, but there was nothing about it that spoke to me. I stood inside the dark cluttered building, and it was as if I were resting, idling, conserving energy for a more strenuous enterprise to come.

A moment later, I had walked around the back of the house, crossed through the tangled brush and crumbling stone walls in the gathering dusk, and had come to stand next to the house on the far side, just below my old bedroom window.

My father's heavy footsteps on the stairs had wakened me. He swung open the bedroom door and I knew instantly, as if I had been standing downstairs in the kitchen between my mother and father, what had happened between them when she had returned from my room armed with my betrayal, and with utter clarity and an almost welcoming acceptance, I knew what would happen now between him and me.

Violence produces white light and heat inside the head, and it happens both to the person who administers the beating and to the person who is beaten. It is never dark and cold. It happens at the instant of violent contact, before pain is felt, or fear, even, or guilt, so that pain, fear, and guilt come to be seen as merely the price one pays afterwards for this extraordinary immolation. It's as if violence were a gift worth any price. Beyond the light and heat, it's a gift that engenders gorgeous dreams of retribution that last for tens of generations of fathers and children, husbands and wives—it shapes and drives fantasies of becoming huge as a glacier and hard as iron, fast as light and sudden, like a volcano.

When you are hit in the head or slammed in the ribs and thrown to the floor by a powerful man, you find instantly that you are already halfway into a narrative that portrays your return to that moment, a narrative whose primary function is to provide reversal: to make the child into the man, the weak into the strong, the bad into the good. Listen to me: you are locked into that narrative, and no other terms, except those present at its inception, at the very opening of the drama, are available for the reversal—and, oh! when that happens, I have risen up from my narrow bed in the upstairs corner room I shared with my brother in Tobyhanna in 1952, and I overwhelm my dead father's rage with an awful crippling rage of my own.

I eventually moved away from that spot beneath the window of the bedroom and got into my car and drove back to Tobyhanna and then on down to East Stroudsburg University, where that evening I gave my lecture to a small gathering of students and teachers, who seemed appreciative and expressed it with good-natured gentle applause. Afterwards, we ate and drank a little wine in a local restaurant, and I drove home to New York.

I will not go back to the house in Tobyhanna or to the

bar in town, just as after having been there once I have not returned to any of the other houses we lived in when I was growing up, or to the apartments and barrooms in Florida and Boston and New Hampshire, where I first learned the need to protect other people from myself, people who loved me, male and female, and utter strangers, male and female. I go back to each, one time only, and I stand silently outside a window or a door, and I deliberately play back the horrible events that took place there. Then I move on.

I have traveled a lot in recent years, and consequently I have completed almost all my journeys now. When I have returned to every place where someone beat me or I beat someone, when there is no place left to go back to, then for the rest of my life I will have only my memories, these stories, to go to for the heat, for the light, for the awful endlessly recurring end of it.

R U S S E L L   B A N K S

Banks is often said to write about the dark side of the human condition; what he knows so well is the soul of the blue-collar working man who is jammed up, has no place to go with his despair as he walks out each morning, caught in demands of life he cannot act upon.

This dark side is one form of the American experience, as Banks so ably renders in the inarticulate heroes/ antiheroes of his stories.

His recent novels, Continental Drift *and* Affliction, *go deeper still into the hang-ups of that working man, veering into violence due to an inability to alter his condition. As the Rilke poem about the archaic torso of*

Apollo concludes, "You must change your life"—a conclusion echoed in the fiction of Banks.

Banks's other fiction works include Searching for Survivors, Family Life, Hamilton Stark, The Book of Jamaica, Trailerpark, *and others.*

TIGHTS

TIGHTS

Rob Beckham

THE MOVIE WAS SUP-
POSED TO BE MAMA'S TREAT BUT AT THE LAST MIN-
ute Mother would not let her pay for it. "Give her her money
back," Mother said to the girl in the booth. After this was
done, Mother shooed us into the theatre like chickens, send-
ing us ahead to get good seats while she bought popcorn.
"Not too close," she called after us. Mama led me to the third
row. We sat, leaving a seat between us. I started to tell her
that we were too close but she smiled and put a finger to her
lips. Mother came down the aisle. She loomed over me.
"Now, Belle, don't make a scene," Mama said. Mother said,
"Oh, phooey," and plunked herself down between us. Her
name was Annabelle; shortening it made her see red. The
brown paper bag of popcorn was nestled in her lap. We all
reached at the same time. Mock battles ensued. Once she got
over her pique, Mother laughed and slapped our hands.

"Shame on you two," she whispered loudly, "just like two kids."

I called my grandmother "Mama" because that's what she asked to be called. Mother did not think it was that simple. "She made *me* call her 'sister,'" she said, "Mother just can't stand getting old."

The lights dimmed. We watched Movietone News. Our soldiers were fighting their way toward the Chinese border in North Korea. We saw Elizabeth Taylor walk down the aisle to marry Nicky Hilton and then Senator McCarthy waved a piece of paper in the air and said there were Communists in the State Department. Meanwhile, people in California were twirling hula hoops.

"I'd die to go to California," Mama whispered.

"You'd die if you did," Mother whispered back, "they have earthquakes out there."

"You're no fun," Mama said.

The curtains closed, then opened again immediately. A nearly naked, muscular man struck a huge, glittering gong.

J. Arthur Rank Presents, A Production of the Archers.
THE RED SHOES

Color by Technicolor. Blazing, eye-searing Technicolor.

I forgot the popcorn. I forgot Mama and Mother. I became the imperious Boris Lermontov *and* the talented Victoria Page. I spoke Russian and French and English with an English accent. I smoked cigarettes and wrung my hands in despair. My eyes blazed.

"Why do you want to dance?"

"Why do you want to live?"

I was in London, Paris, Monte Carlo—not Berwyn, Maryland. I travelled in train compartments wearing hats as big as the room. I strolled about with a silver-handled cane, wore dark glasses, and stabbed people with words. I was altogether transported until the end. The end I could not agree with. If I'd been Victoria Page, I would have danced forever and never for a moment considered killing myself for a selfish, cold-hearted man like Julian Craster. He reminded me of my father.

"I don't usually like foreign pictures," Mother said, wiping the tears from her eyes.

"Lord, honey, you better use my hanky," Mama said to me.

"I will be a great dancer," I announced without a moment's hesitation.

"Now wait just a minute," Mother said.

"Well, I suppose it's a free country," Mama said, "why only last week he was going to swallow swords, and you had no objection to that."

This was true, but it was also last week. Now I had a real calling.

Mother frowned. "Let's keep this one under our hat," she said, "unless you want Arch to go through the roof."

My father was playing golf the Sunday that we saw *The Red Shoes*. It was Dawson's turn to carry his bag. My brother and I took turns. He was paid two dollars for eighteen holes, I was paid a dollar. Dawson was fifteen, able to bear the weight. For me, at eleven, the bag was quite a load and made all the heavier by the disparity in our wages. However, it was useless to protest. My father insisted that Dawson had better uses for the money. He was a Senior Scout, never missed a meeting; he planned on joining De-Molay as well; he saved for things like slide rules, star maps, and baseball cards, which were just then coming into vogue. Moreover, he was an attentive caddy, nudging Dad to use an iron when he was inclined to favor one of the lesser woods. Afterward he was eager to challenge Dad on the putting green, using the extra putter that Dad had for just that purpose. By contrast, my expenditures were thought frivolous, if not worse. I bought jacks and became quite adept. I sent away for the rubber sword referred to by Mama and made several attempts to swallow it before realizing that proficiency necessarily involved a good deal of retching and, on one occasion, the loss of lunch. My most recent purchase had been a white rayon scarf that I pretended was silk. (On my way home from the movie that Sunday it suddenly occurred to me that Boris Lermontov would wear such a garment. In fact I convinced myself that he would never be seen without it.) When it came to caddying I was hopeless. I never learned one club from the other, or, more accurately, I refused to learn their differences. When Dad said, "Hand me the four iron," I hauled forth the number two wood. When his ball landed in the rough, I caused distraction by picking dandelions or shooting hard-stemmed weeds. I always lagged behind, never cleaned his balls to his satisfaction, and when the nightmare was finally over (barring a tie which meant extra holes but no extra pay), I waited by the car instead of fraternizing with the other caddies. My loathing for his favorite game was an affront he never forgave.

After the movie, we saw Mama to her apartment, then Mother and I walked the short distance home. We paused in the park to seesaw, Mother riding side-saddle because she was wearing a skirt. As she went up in the air she said, "How would you like to take piano lessons? Gretchen wants to sell her piano and I was thinking I might want to learn too."

"No thanks," I said.

Back up in the air again, she said, "Why not? I bet you'd be good."

"Maybe," I said, "but I'm going to be a dancer." She jumped off the seesaw but held the board so that I hit the ground with just the slightest bump.

"We can't afford the lessons," she said.

"Piano lessons cost too."

"All right," she said, "we both know it's your father. It would be like waving a red flag in front of a bull."

"Why?"

"What happened when Milton Berle did *Swan Lake?*"

What happened was this: my father, who seldom laughed out loud and never cried except when reading the Bible, did both. When Uncle Miltie also shouted "Makeup!" his glee became a paroxysm. Whether incarnated in tights or tutu, Milton Berle was Dad's idea of "the perfect fairy."

"We don't have to tell him," I suggested.

Mother shook her head. "I don't keep secrets from your father," she said.

That evening I appeared at dinner as Boris Lermontov. I tied my white rayon scarf as an ascot and wore it beneath my one and only long-sleeved white shirt. There was nothing unusual in my coming to dinner as someone else, though heretofore my persona was imagined rather than costumed for the part. My unsuspecting family had dined with King Arthur, Little Lord Fauntleroy, and Ozma of Oz, to name just a few. As we shared the same bedroom, Dawson frequently knew of my current infatuation. He mocked me, hid my books, chased me about the room with my own rubber sword, and on one occasion informed the family that my refusal to speak was not remorse at the miserable report card I'd brought home that afternoon.

"He's Sleeping Beauty," Dawson said with great disgust. "Look, he's eating with his eyes closed."

My eyes snapped open. I had been attempting to eat

with them closed, and I was pretending to be the comatose princess, but self-preservation made me say, "You're a liar. I was pretending to be blind."

While I was in thrall to Boris Lermontov that night, Dad read the newspaper. He was a short man, wiry and athletic. He wore an undershirt that showed his muscular arms. Beads of sweat glistened where his dark brown hair had begun to recede. Mother wore shorts and a halter; her blond hair was swept up in a bandana. Dawson asked and obtained permission to appear at the table in his bathing suit. All the windows were wide open but there was no breeze. I felt perspiration gathering in the center of my chest; it was already running down my arms.

"I guess you haven't read the paper," Dad said. He held up the front section: WASHINGTON AREA MELTS UNDER RECORD HEAT WAVE.

I shrugged and continued eating tuna noodle casserole.

Dawson laughed. "Who are you this time?" he asked. I gave him a withering look.

"Honey, you must be burning up," Mother said.

"I do not feel za heat," I said, doing my best to sound like Boris.

"Get outta here," said Dawson.

"We saw *The Red Shoes* this afternoon," Mother said. "I think Steve's gone overboard for this Russian guy . . ."

"Russian," Dad interrupted, "you mean Communist?"

Mother laughed. "No, no. Hold your horses. He ran a . . ." She paused for just a second. "Well, he ran this, uh, dance company."

Dad looked at me. "Get upstairs and take that thing off your neck and change your shirt."

I did not move.

"Did you hear me?"

"Arch," Mother began.

"Not now, Annabelle," he said. "I said MOVE!"

I moved.

Now, of course, I realize that I was a fairly absurd child. Had I pretended to be Babe Ruth or Ben Hogan, my parents could have congratulated themselves on a job well done, or, had I chosen to impersonate less well-defined characters, that is, shown more originality, I might have staked a claim to true comic genius and perhaps baffled my father into treating me with some kind of respect. What puzzled me and made me so inwardly defiant was the fact that I could make others laugh but never him. If I brought a smile to his face there was always something grim about it.

By the following Christmas I had tired of Boris Lermontov; his white-hot intensity was difficult to sustain. As for the aristocratic Victoria Page, I found nothing in Mother's simple wardrobe that even remotely suggested that lady. I looked ridiculous in Mother's tiny, head-hugging hats, and she did not wear high heels, for that would have made her taller than my father. She was also, at this time, keen with suspicion, accurately surmising my responsibility for the occasional disorder in her closet. She never actually caught me, but she threatened to tell my father if she ever did. In any event, I was, if I remember correctly, alternating my impression of Boris with the Errol Flynn version of the Earl of Essex. My scarf became a sash into which I inserted the rubber sword. I was constantly "On Guard!" This particular characterization evoked mild approval from Dad. He said that a boyhood desire of his was to be like General J.E.B. Stuart, dashing hero of the Confederacy, who bedecked himself not only with sash and sword but with ostrich feathers for his hat.

"Oh, God," Mother groaned, "did you have to say that?"

She did not need to worry. I had absolutely no interest in the history of the United States.

During the two-week Christmas vacation, Mama introduced another element into our delicate family equation. She was eager to parade her new friend, David Young. They came to dinner New Year's Eve. He was tall, thin, and pale with a long, straight nose, a cleft chin, and a forelock of blond hair that kept falling over his right eye. For some reason my father asked him how old he was, and he said he was twenty-five.

"A babe in the woods," Mama said. She smiled at him the way she often smiled at me. "On Guard!" Mama supplied the information that David lived on the third floor of her apartment building and taught art at the high school.

"It's my first year," he said. "I should have been a policeman."

"How's that?" Dad asked. He was slicing roast beef. David Young had asked for "the pinkest you've got," but Dad said, "It's all well done."

"A lot of rednecks take art because they think it's a snap," he said. "They carve up the desks with the Exacto knife. I get almost photographic renditions of guns, spears, and bayonets, but I got reported to the school board for showing them a picture of the Daveed."

"The what?" Dad asked.

"David by Michelangelo," he said. "They better have all their clothes on if you want to work in this state."

"Well, it's hard to see what's wrong with that," Mother said.

I watched David Young look quickly at Mama, then back at his plate. Mama winked at me. I wasn't sure what was going on but it felt good to be part of it. Dad cleared his throat. "What do you think of the Redskins?"

David Young brushed his hair back. "To be honest," he said, "I'm not up on baseball."

"Baseball!" Dawson was outraged. "Boy, that's rich."

After that Dad acted like we'd all disappeared from the table. He finished his dinner and went into the living room. A minute or so later Dawson joined him in front of our new television.

"I don't understand modern art," Mother said while she cleared the table.

"I don't either," said David Young. "I look at pictures hoping I'll feel something."

"Like what?"

"Oh, I don't know. Joy, maybe, pain, sadness, passion, things like that."

"Don't tell me you get any of that out of black and blue blobs."

"Now, Belle," Mama said, "what about dessert?"

"In a few minutes . . ."

"If they're watching wrestling I'm going home."

"The Redskins are a football team," I said to David Young.

He smiled, looking directly at me. "Who cares?" he said. I thought about that for just a second, then I smiled back. I remember the pleasure of that smile; it turned my face red.

"Who are you kidding?" Mother said to Mama while I was talking to David Young. "I've seen you watching those wrestlers between your fingers."

"I'd rather play Hearts," Mama said. She turned to me. "Honey, go ask Arch if he wants to play cards." Hearts was a game Dad loved to play. He was always "shooting the moon," savoring our defeat by saying things like, "cream rises to the top," or "class shows every time."

"Kill him," Dawson said to our ten-inch television, where Gorgeous George lay spread-eagled under Antonio Rocca.

"Never happen," said Dad. He flicked ashes off his cigar and for the first time noticed me.

"Mama wants to play Hearts," I said.

"Not with that jerk," Dawson whispered.

"Maybe after this," said Dad.

"We're leaving," Mama said after I told her no cards. "I've got a bottle of champagne and better things to do than squint at that little box."

"Can I come too?" I asked her.

She shrugged. "No harm in asking," she said.

I went into the kitchen. "Ask your father," Mother said. After Hearts, our next favorite game was Passing the Buck. I went back into the living room.

"What now?" Dad asked.

"They're leaving and I want to walk them home."

"Ask your mother."

"She said to ask you."

"For cryin' out loud, we're watching T.V.," Dawson said.

"Stay home. Help with the dishes."

"It's his turn," I said, glaring at my brother.

"I don't care," Dad exploded, "just don't bother me now."

When they left, my father stood up, shook David Young's hand, but did not look at him or wish him Happy

New Year. He kissed Mama on the cheek. She said, "Happy New Year, you old fogey."

I also shook his hand after I kissed Mama. I walked out on the porch with them. He took Mama's arm to help her down the front steps. I rushed forward and grabbed her other one.

"I feel like Queen Elizabeth," Mama said.

David smiled but his voice became gruff, mocking. "We'll have to toss the pigskin around sometime, huh buddy?"

I got that same flushed feeling in my face. "So long," he called over his shoulder.

"You'll catch your death," Mother called from inside.

"That guy doesn't know his ass from second base," Dawson said after the door was closed.

Dad blew a smoke ring. My brother stuck a finger through it.

"Who wants peach cobbler?" Mother asked.

David Young spent three Saturdays in January painting Mama's portrait. First he did a sketch in charcoal, then switched to watercolors. I liked the charcoal drawing so much he gave it to me. Mama sat in her favorite chair, which was slipcovered in bright red cabbage roses. Behind her on the windowsill were her houseplants, including a beautiful purplish-white gloxinia that she knew the secret of bringing back year after year. Sugar, her green and yellow parakeet, also appeared in the picture, along with the polychrome Kwan Yin that Mother so admired she once threatened to steal it. I sulked at first because I felt left out. David Young made Mama sit still; he would not allow her to read to me. When she fell asleep he threatened to paint her with *three* chins. We could not listen to "Let's Pretend" on the radio because "an artist needs to concentrate." Before long, however, I became enthralled at her emergence there on the paper. Her auburn, almost red, hair was just right, her comfortable, handsome face did have a slight double chin, and he caught her drooping eyelids, which I'm sure in another era she would have corrected with plastic surgery. He was so talented I let my bladder fill to bursting rather than leave them alone for a moment. I pretended absorption in *Stuart Little*. I read the same sentence so often I can reproduce it from memory: "The doctor was delighted with Stuart and said that it was very unusual for an American family to have a mouse." They must have been amused at such unrelenting surveillance.

Early in February David's drawing, now entitled "I Remember Mama," won first prize in the sixth grade Original Art Contest. Miss Hart, my teacher, said, "I had no idea you had such talent." I blushed modestly. Phyliss Rosenberg, no doubt upset that her rendition of "Moses and the Burning Bush" had garnered only second place, said, "I bet he didn't do it."

For once I kept my mouth shut.

"You'll apologize right this minute, young lady," said Miss Hart.

Phyliss caved in. "I'm sorry," she said, but the defiant, sidelong look in her eye told me she was anything but. Ever since the Rosenbergs (no relation that I know of) had been convicted of treason and sentenced to the electric chair, I'd been calling her a Communist. On the way home from school that day I caught up to her, and, waving the drawing with its blue ribbon in her face, I chanted a poem of my own creation: "Julius and Ethel sat in the chair/ The switch was pulled and they lost all their hair."

"Liar, sissy, son-of-a-bitch," she said, followed by, "I

wish you were dead." Before I could stop her, she tore the drawing out of my hand and ripped it to shreds.

I chased her, but to no avail; her feet were inspired by crime.

Sometime in March my interest in the dance was unexpectedly revived, thanks to David Young. He and Mama went on expeditions to Washington, D.C., and on the Saturdays when Dawson was Dad's caddy or bad weather prevented either one of us from carrying his bag, I was free to go along. We spent a lot of time in the National Gallery of Art and the museums along the Mall. We went to movies in the theatres on F Street and window-shopped along Connecticut Avenue. It was on one of these walks along Connecticut Avenue that I spied a clutch of tutued little girls. They wore coats, scarves, and mittens over their pure white tulle.

"Aha!" said David, seeing them at the same time, "budding ballerinas." Giggling, and no doubt scared to death, these girls were entering a mansion over whose columned portico a bright red banner proclaimed: The National Ballet of Washington. A sign on the door read: Student Rehearsal of Act II, Swan Lake, Open to the Public. I dragged Mama and David inside.

"I'm starved," Mama said, "wouldn't you rather have Chinese food?"

"Have a heart," David said, "just look at this house."

The foyer had black-and-white marble floors, gold-leafed corinthian columns, and a huge crystal chandelier that Mama said she'd hate to have to clean. In the well of a spiral staircase two women in hats sat behind a table selling tickets for fifty cents apiece.

David put his hands on my shoulders. "My son is a ballet student in New York," he said to one of the women.

"Any reciprocity for fellow artists?"

"You don't look old enough to be anyone's father," the woman said.

"It's a curse," said David.

I got in free.

We walked up the staircase to the ballroom—or rather Mama, David, and a reborn Boris Lermontov did. This house, despite faded walls and water-damaged cornices, had all the grandeur of Lady Neston's London home where Lermontov first met her niece, Victoria Page.

We sat on wooden folding chairs in the fourth row. Mama sighed. "Shrimp fried rice," she whispered to David. The scenery was two free-standing trees—one fell over during the performance—painted marsh grasses, a lake of course, and drinking from it, two fawns. Screens painted with both black and white swans had been erected on either side to permit unseen entrances and exits and to hide the Victrola.

There were too many cygnets to hide behind the screens once the scratchy music began. They entered from both sides without mishap, but their exits resembled highway pileups. As the exits had been staged according to the swans' height, the smallest girls were left high and dry on stage. Several burst into tears, and one broke down and wailed for "Mommy." The others jostled the Victrola, causing the music to race ahead of the action. Mama missed all this, for she had fallen asleep within the first five minutes. David's face became the color of an azalea; he gripped the sides of his chair and squeezed his eyes so tight tears rolled down his cheeks. I laughed, too, but the Lermontov in me was outraged. Though I had no basis of comparison, never having seen a live performance of anything, I knew that Foster Mayberry, the Prince, was awful. He was skinny, had pimples, and could hardly lift the Swan Queen, danced by Annie Redd Fontaine. I scoffed at his leaps, laughed when he staggered under the Queen, and did not applaud when he appeared for a solo bow. This all stemmed from my absolute conviction that I would have danced rings around them both and been rewarded with a standing ovation.

At the end there was a standing ovation. All the little swans rushed into the welcoming arms of their parents and I heard them say, "You were wonderful." "The real star of the show." I even heard Foster Mayberry's father say, "We're proud of you, son." Mama woke up. "Thank God!" she said. We walked down the staircase and I remember wishing I'd been wearing a train. I had to use the bathroom. Mama said, "Hurry up. I'm ready to pass out from hunger." I went down into the basement, opened the door, and there stood Foster Mayberry, wearing nothing but what I now know is called a "dancer's belt."

"Get out!" he said, his pimply face becoming livid. "This is my dressing room." He darted into the single stall and slammed the door. On the floor were the white tights he'd worn as the Prince. I scooped them up, shoved them inside my coat, and ran out the door. I bolted up the stairs, grabbed Mama's hand.

"Let's go," I said. My heart did not stop racing until we were seated in a red plastic booth at the Shanghai Palace, blocks away on M Street. It was warm but I could not take off my coat.

"I hope you're not coming down with something," Mama said.

David put his palm on my forehead. "Swan fever," he said.

The tights had to be washed, for I was fastidious by nature. Also, at this time, I harbored the conviction that pimples were contagious. However, I couldn't just slip them in the wash because Mother put everything through the wringer. I snuck into the bathroom and rinsed them out with Dial deodorant soap, then hung them to dry in the attic. I was very pleased with myself that evening. Secrets are invigorating, especially when you have reason to believe that no one on earth could possibly guess them. I whistled and sang snatches of "Have You Heard?", the latest hit by Joni James.

"Only queers can whistle," said Dawson, voicing a strange, persistent belief among his peers. (He also thought that queers invariably wore pink on Thursday.) I'm sure we traded insults, we usually did, but that night I was preoccupied with the cartwheel and learning to do a back-bend by inching my hands down the wall. Not for me the stiff postures of a Foster Mayberry. I would bring something new to the dance.

Being sick was the only way to skip church on Sunday mornings. At breakfast I gagged on the hotcakes and shot up the stairs. I pretended to retch, then flushed the toilet quickly so all Mother saw was a wad of paper disappearing down the bowl. My temperature was perfectly normal, but she allowed me to stay in bed anyway.

After the front door closed, I counted to two hundred, then jumped out of bed. The tights were not quite dry, but I heaved and stretched myself into them nonetheless. They felt like a second skin. I threw off my pajama tops, tied the white scarf around my waist, and barefoot and bare-chested, ran downstairs. We had one classical record, José Iturbi playing Rachmaninoff's "Second Piano Concerto." I listened for a moment but soon became utterly exultant—leaping, turning, rushing from room to room only to halt, hide behind the living room curtains, and then spring forward again. The music seemed made for noble attitudes, one after another; it was as if my chin sought to reach the ceiling. Mother's oval hooked rug became a nest of snakes with whom I engaged in mortal combat. I writhed on the floor and slithered down the walls and all the while my mind kept inventing stories in which I danced away from evil in all its guises.

And I almost got caught. I heard Dawson yelling to Ken Carney that he'd be right over. I stopped the phonograph, shut the top, and raced upstairs. I must have left an energy field behind because Mother came right up.

"Quit pretending to be asleep," she said. Then, apparently taking a closer look, she said, "My God, you're covered with sweat." I "awoke" from feverish slumber. This time my temperature was elevated by a degree. While she returned to the bathroom to break an aspirin, I peeled off the tights and stuffed them under the mattress.

For some reason she suspected appendicitis. She wanted to feel my abdomen, but I clutched the sheets because I had nothing on underneath.

"You haven't been . . . well, you know, have you?"

"What?" I really did not know what she had in mind.

"I mean, fooling around."

Of course I'd been fooling around, but obviously not in the way she meant—that kind of fooling around was two years in the future. Now I sensed a definite advantage through her embarrassment.

"Fooling around how?"

"Your father will just have to explain. I shouldn't have to."

I knew she was talking about something "dirty" just by the way she refused to talk about it. However, if she brought Dad into the picture, her false accusation might become a fact and this could involve the razor strap again.

"I was not fooling around," I said. "I swear on a stack of Bibles."

"So you *do* know what I mean," she said.

"No, I don't know what you mean," I said. "I was not fooling around." I said this with such conviction she believed me.

"Okay," she said. "When I leave you get up and put your pajamas on and get back in bed. I'll bring you some orange juice later. Let's see, is it feed a fever and starve a cold or vice versa?"

After she left I counted to fifty. I pulled the tights from under the mattress, tiptoed to the closet, and stuffed them into the sleeve of a Sunday school jacket I'd recently outgrown. When she returned I was absorbed in *Forever Amber*.

On Easter Sunday, as I got dressed for church I noticed that the jacket was missing. I searched frantically, went through Dawson's clothes, and then turned my back and told myself that when I looked again there the jacket would be, but it was nowhere to be found.

"I'm counting to ten," Dad yelled up the stairs.

I searched their faces and thought I detected something different in Mother's expression, but I could not be sure. We went to church and there my habitual fidgets were considerably augmented by the awful thrill of possible discovery. We sat in a pew with Aunt Thelma, Uncle Dwight, and my cousin Willis. They came home with us for afternoon dinner. Aunt Thelma was Dad's only sister, and they looked a lot alike. He livened up around her. Mother said the two of them together made her feel like she wasn't in the room. Uncle Dwight had the ability to fall asleep with one eye open. Aunt Thelma said it was "his trick." He never said much because she would not let him get a word in edgewise. Willis was Dawson's age. His acne was worse than Foster Mayberry's. He carried a penknife in one sock. To Dawson's great delight, he threatened to cut my balls off after dinner. Needless to say, we had absolutely nothing in common.

Mama showed up just before we sat down to eat. She never went to church. "I can't be bothered," she said once when I asked her why not. "It's either too hot or too cold, or it's raining or snowing or I just get the strongest feeling that the Lord is saying, 'Honey, roll over and go back to sleep.' "

I sat between her and Uncle Dwight. As usual, he had two Cokes and a glass of ice in front of him. He'd drink at least six of them before falling asleep, waking up, and starting all over again. Right then Aunt Thelma was laughing about her brother-in-law, Burden, whose oldest daughter was engaged to a man with the last name of Weed. "Spelled just like one," she said.

"How would you feel about having a 'Weed' in your family?" she asked my father.

"I have one already," he said.

"Me too," Aunt Thelma said, squeezing Willis's neck, "he sure is growing like one. What kind of television did you get?" she asked without a pause.

"Motorola," Mother said.

"Don't you just love that Imogene Coca?" Aunt Thelma asked.

"I hate that woman," Dad said. "She's ugly as a mud fence and she isn't funny."

"Oh, for pity sake, Arch, you must be made of stone. She's got that rubber mouth and those teeth! I think she's the most comical woman alive. Tell him he's full of beans, Annabelle."

"You tell him," Mother said. "To be honest, I think

Martha Raye has her beat in the mouth department."

"Getting back to weeds," Mama said, "if you had to be one, which would it be?"

"Clover," Uncle Dwight said, "I'd like to be rolling in clover."

"Clover's not a weed," said Aunt Thelma. "I'd be a wild Irish rose."

"You mean Wild Turkey," Willis said. My father and Dawson hooted at that. Mother smiled behind her napkin. "I think a jack-in-the-pulpit . . ."

"Belle," Mama interrupted, "I said *weeds*, not wildflowers."

"This is nuts," said Dad. "Pass that ham over here."

"I know what you'd be sure enough," Mama said, smiling at him.

"What?"

"Skunk cabbage!"

I was like a train plunging from a broken trestle. Mama sensed it; she squeezed my thigh so hard under the table I suddenly realized that I was the only one still laughing. My father finished dinner with a tight little smile around his lips. Aunt Thelma continued talking, but nothing she said got a rise out of Dad. I recall helping with the dishes and afterward playing several games of croquet. In the joy they took at knocking my ball to kingdom come, Dawson and Willis forgot their intention of cutting mine off after supper.

An hour or so before dark, rain drove us inside. While Uncle Dwight slept, the rest of us played Hearts. Dad won. Mama beat me by five points for last place. Just before the "Ed Sullivan Show," Mother served a second dessert, peach cobbler again. She asked me to help. As she dished the cobbler she said, "Steve, I want to . . ." but Aunt Thelma popped in, telling us to get a move on because the show had already started.

The guests that night included Morey Amsterdam, Vic Damone, Helen Traubel, and the American Indian ballerina Maria Tallchief, doing an excerpt from, what else? *Swan Lake*. Just before her appearance, my father suddenly got up and moved his chair back from in front of the television. "Clear a path there," he said to Aunt Thelma. "Give me room, boys," he said to Dawson and Willis. "I'll be right back." With that he hurried from the room and I heard him run up the stairs. On television, the curtains parted and there stood Maria Tallchief, surrounded by her swans. As the music began Dad yelled, "Hang on, I'm coming!"

"What is going on?" Aunt Thelma asked.

"I've no idea," Mama said.

Dad leaped into the living room, dressed in my white tights and wearing the white scarf around his head like a turban. He gyrated like a hula girl, his face distorted. He extended his arms like Maria Tallchief was doing on television, he tried to stand on tiptoes. As she fled, so did he, adding a few Indian war whoops as he sped from the room, through the kitchen and the dining room, before confronting us once again. The tights had split up the right side, the turban came undone, to be used as a banner on his next circuit of the house. Dawson and Willis rolled on the floor. Aunt Thelma held her sides. "I never," she kept repeating. I remained rigid, my hands under my legs.

"What the hell is this?" Uncle Dwight asked, waking from Coke-induced stupor. Nobody answered his question, though I could have and so could my mother. I looked at her. She wasn't laughing, but she would not look back. Finally, when Tallchief was through, so was my father. He mimicked her curtain call before racing back upstairs.

I dreaded his return, but when he did and Aunt Thelma asked him what it was all about, he said, "Oh, nothing. I just felt like dancing."

That summer we got lost in the Pentagon parking lot. Instead of playing golf, Dad took our new car, a bright red two-door, bullet-nosed Studebaker, for a Sunday drive. Once inside the lot Dad agreed that Dawson could take a turn at the wheel.

"Are you sure?" Mother asked.

"Does he have a permit?" Mama wanted to know.

"No," I whispered to her.

Dad stopped the car and got out. Dawson was out of the backseat like a shot. Mother climbed in with us.

"No backseat driving," Dad warned. "Okay, son, easy does it."

We lurched forward. Mama groaned. I wanted her to groan louder.

Dawson drove us deeper into the lot. It had many sections, ramps, sawhorse barricades, an infinity of grass-planted islands studded with skimpy-looking trees, and roads marked "Exit" that led nowhere. I have to admit that Dawson was a born driver. After the initial hesitation, he steered us around as if he'd been driving all his life. However, after twenty minutes or so a palpable claustrophobia seized everyone but him.

"I'm getting carsick," Mama said.

"Yes," Mother agreed, "it's time to get out of here."

"Five more minutes," Dawson pleaded.

"Better pull over," Dad said. "You did great."

We spent the better part of an hour trying to escape the Pentagon. Mother pointed out a possible route. Mama suggested the opposite direction. I said nothing. Dawson said he'd decided to go for Explorer Scout.

"Start by getting us out of here!" Mother snapped.

Finally we spotted a guard asleep in his patrol car. "It happens all the time," he said, rubbing his eyes. He started his engine and led us out.

No one said a word as we headed toward Memorial Bridge. Dad drove us around the Lincoln Memorial and then circled it again until he found a place to park. Mama claimed her legs were dead after being hauled out by Mother. We strolled the length of the Reflecting Pool, slimy green with algae and dotted with litter. Mother wondered what kind of people would trash a national monument. Mama said, "Lord, Belle, you've answered your own question." She rested on a bench and told us to holler for her after we had our look at Abraham Lincoln.

At least three hundred other people were milling about inside the monument. We posed, necks craned; there he sat, The Great Emancipator.

Dad slipped one arm around Mother's waist, the other was draped over Dawson's shoulder. Mother's arms were around my neck.

"We live in a great country," Dad said.

"That's right," Mother agreed, hugging me. Then, in the same reverential tone, she felt moved to add, "And the best part is that you can be anything you want to be."

R O B   B E C K H A M

Nine years ago, Rob Beckham's father phoned him to talk about the letters Rob had written about his experiences as a squad leader in the U.S. Army.

"Son," said the elder Beckham, "I laughed so hard I wet my pants. You ought to be a writer."

Rob answered, "Yeah, goddammit," to which his father replied, "Now don't take the Lord's name in vain, just write like you do in your letters."

Here is his first published story, and it is a pleasure to publish it and be part of his debut.

We hope his father is pleased.

Rob now lives in West Hollywood, writing, and has, we hear, completed more stories.

A CITIZEN READS
THE CONSTITUTION

A CITIZEN READS
THE CONSTITUTION

E. L. Doctorow

OT INCLUDING THE
AMENDMENTS, IT IS APPROXIMATELY 5,000 WORDS
long—about the length of a short story. It is an enigmatically
dry, unemotional piece of work, tolling off in its monotone
the structures and functions of government, the conditions
and obligations of office, the limitations of powers, the means
for redressing crimes and conducting commerce. It makes
itself the supreme law of the land. It concludes with instructions on how it can amend itself, and undertakes to pay all
the debts incurred by the states under its indigent parent,
the Articles of Confederation.

It is no more scintillating as reading than I remember it
to have been in Mrs. Brundage's seventh-grade civics class
at Joseph H. Wade Junior High School. It is 5,000 words but
reads like 50,000. It lacks high rhetoric and shows not a
trace of wit, as you might expect, having been produced by a
committee of lawyers. It uses none of the tropes of literature

to create empathetic states in the mind of the reader. It does not mean to persuade. It abhors metaphor as nature abhors a vacuum.

One's first reaction upon reading it is to rush for relief to an earlier American document, as alive with passion and the juices of outrage as the work of any single artist:

> We hold these truths to be self-evident, that all men are created equal, that they are endowed by their Creator with certain unalienable Rights, that among these are Life, Liberty and the pursuit of Happiness. That to secure these rights, Governments are instituted among Men, deriving their just powers from the consent of the governed. That whenever any Form of Government becomes destructive of these ends, it is the Right of the People to alter or to abolish it, and to institute new Government.

Here is the substantive diction of a single human mind—Thomas Jefferson's, as it happens—even as it speaks for all. It is engaged in the art of literary revolution, rewriting history, overthrowing divine claims to rule and genealogical hierarchies of human privilege as cruel frauds, defining human rights as universal and distributing the source and power of government to the people governed. It is the radical voice of national liberation, combative prose lifting its musketry of self-evident truths and firing away.

What reader does not wish the Constitution could have been written out of something of the same spirit? Of course, we all know instinctively that it could not, that statue-writing in the hands of lawyers has its own demands, and those are presumably precision and clarity, which call for sentences bolted at all four corners with *wherein*'s and *whereunder*'s and *thereof*'s and *therein*'s and notwith-standing the *foregoing*'s.

Still and all, our understanding of the Constitution must come of an assessment of its character as a composition, and it would serve us to explore further why it is the way it is. Here is something of what I have learned of the circumstances under which it was written.

THE BACKGROUND

The Constitutional Convention was called in the first place because in the postwar world of North America influential men in the government, in the Continental Congress, were not confident that the loosely structured Articles of Confederation, as written, could make permanent the gains of the Revolution. Without the hated British to unite them the states would revert to bickering and mutual exploitation. They had as many problems with one another as the classes of people in each state had among themselves, and men like George Washington and James Madison foresaw a kind of anarchy ensuing that would lead to yet another despotism, either native or from foreign invasion by the Spanish or again by the English. Many competing interests were going unmediated. The agrarian Southern states, with their tropical rice and cotton plantations, saw danger to themselves in export taxes applied to all their goods by the North Atlantic port states. The small states, like Delaware, felt threatened by their bigger neighbors, such as Pennsylvania. There was immense debt as a result of the Revolution, which debtors wanted to pay off with state-issued paper money—and which creditors, security holders, bankers, merchants, men of wealth, wanted returned in hard currency. There were diverse ethnic and religious communities, black slaves, white indentured servants. And there were Indians in the woods. The states not contiguous had little in common with one another. To the New Yorker, South Carolina was not the South; it was another kingdom entirely, with people of completely different backgrounds and with bizarre manners in speech and deportment—foreigners, in short. Georgia and South Carolina depended on slave labor to run their plantations. Slavery was abhorrent to many Northerners in 1787, and an economy of slaves was morally detestable.

It is important to remind ourselves in this regard that Colonial society had existed for 150 years before the idea of independence caught on. That's a long time, certainly long enough for an indigenous class of great wealth to arise and a great schism to emerge between the rich and the poor. A very few people owned most of the land and were keenly resented. Three percent of the population controlled 50 percent of the wealth. People were not stupid; there was general knowledge of the plunder, legal chicanery, favoritism, privilege of name and corruption of government officials that had created such inequity. In fact, it is possible that organization of public sentiment against King George is exactly what saved the Colonies from tearing themselves apart with insurrections of the poor against the rich; that events like the Boston Tea Party and calls to arms by Jefferson and Tom Paine created the common enemy, the British, to unify all the classes in America and save, by diversion of anger and rage to the redcoats, the fortunes and hides of the American upper class. This was the class, as it happened, of most of the fifty-five men who convened in Philadelphia. Washington was perhaps the largest landowner in the country. Benjamin Franklin possessed a considerable fortune, and Madison owned several slave plantations.

There was an additional factor to make them sensitive. The convention had been called to consider amendments to the Articles of Confederation. The Continental Congress was even now sitting in New York City and doing government business, and not all that ineffectually. It was, for example, passing legislation outlawing slavery in the western territories. But rather than amending the Articles, the convention in Philadelphia was pursuaded to throw them aside entirely and design something new—a federal entity that would incorporate the states. The agenda for this course of action was proposed by Governor Edmund Randolph of Virginia, who presented a number of resolutions for debate, and so it has come to be called the Virginia plan. But the sentiment for something new, a new federal government over and above state sovereignties, had the strong support of influential delegates from several venues. And so the convention got down to business that was actually subversive. It violated its own mandate and began to move in the direction the federalists pushed it. It was because of this and because no one participating wanted, in the vigorous debates that were to ensue over the next months, to be confronted with a record of his remarks or positions, that the conventioneers agreed to make their deliberations secret for the entire time they sat, permitting no official journal of the proceedings and swearing themselves to a press blackout, as it were. That was to upset Jefferson greatly, who was off in France as a minister; the idea of such secrecy repelled him. Only Madison, fortunately for us, kept a notebook, which did not come to light until 1843 but which provides us the fullest account of those secret deliberations and the character of the minds that conducted them.

What a remarkable group of minds they were. The first thing they did was constitute themselves as a Committee of the Whole, which gave them the power of improvisation and debate, flexibility of action, so that when the collected resolutions were decided on they could present them to themselves in plenary session.

Methodically, treating one thorny question after another, they made their stately way through the agenda. If something could not be resolved it was tabled and the next issue was confronted. Nothing stopped their painstaking progress through the maze of ideas and resolutions from which they slowly constructed a new world for themselves: who would make the laws, who would execute them, who would review their judicial propriety; should the small states balk at proportional representation, then the Senate would be created to give equal representation to every state. Some matters were easy to agree on—the writ of *habeas corpus*, the precise nature of treason. If one reads any of the dramatic reconstructions of their work, and there are several good books that provide this, one has the thrill of watching living, fallible men composing the United States of America and producing its ruling concept of federalism, a system of national and local governments, each with defined powers and separate legal jurisdictions.

Through it all Washington sat up at the front of the room, and he never said a word. The less he said the more his prestige grew. They had settled on one chief executive, to be called a President, and everyone knew who it would be. He had only to sit there to give the delegates courage to persevere. Franklin, too, lent the considerable weight of his presence, only occasionally saying a few soft words or passing up a note to be read by the speaker. Franklin was an old man at the time, over 80. At one point, when the proceedings were bogging down in dissension, he offered the recommendation that everyone stop and pray. The lawyers were so stunned by this idea that tempers cooled, probably just as he had intended, and the meeting went on.

And as the weeks wore on there slowly emerged among the delegates—or must have—a rising sense of their identity not only as Carolinians or Virginians or New Yorkers but as American nationals. A continental vision of nationhood lit their minds, and a collaborative excitement had to have come over them as day after day, month after month, they fantasized together their nation on paper. One cannot read any account of their deliberations without understanding how they made things up as they went along from their own debated differences, so that a sort of group intellect arose. It was wise with a knowledge of the way men act with power and from what motives. This objectification of separate personalities and interests came of a unanimous familiarity with parliamentary method and was finally self-propelling. These men invented a country of language, and that language celebrated—whether in resolutions of moral triumph or moral failure—the idea of law. The idea of a dispassionate law ruling men, even those men who were to make and effect the law.

Enough resolutions having been put forth, a Committee of Detail was formed to get them into an orderly shape, and that was accomplished with the scheme of articles, and sections under the articles, grouping the resolutions about legislative, judicial and executive branches, the rights and obligations of the states, the supremacy of the Constitution as law, etc.

When the Committee of Detail had structured the

composition and it was duly examined and considered and amended, a Committee of Style was formed. That is my favorite committee. It comprised William Samuel Johnson of Connecticut, Alexander Hamilton of New York, Madison of Virginia, Rufus King of Massachusetts, and Gouverneur Morris of Pennsylvania. Apparently Morris did the actual writing. And it is this document, produced by the Committee of Style and approved by the convention, that was called the Constitution of the United States. And for the first time in the various drafts there appeared in the preamble the phrase "We the people of the United States," thus quietly absorbing both the seminal idea of the Declaration of Independence and the continental vision of federalism.

THE VOICE OF THE CONSTITUTION

So we come back to this question of text. It is true but not sufficient to say that the Constitution reads as it does because it was written by a committee of lawyers. Something more is going on here. Every written composition has a voice, a persona, a character of presentation, whether by design of the author or not. The voice of the Constitution is a quiet voice. It does not rally us; it does not call on self-evident truths; it does not arm itself with philosophy or political principle; it does not argue, explain, condemn, excuse or justify. It is postrevolutionary. Not claiming righteousness, it is, however, suffused with rectitude. It is this way because it seeks standing in the world, the elevation of the unlawful acts of men—unlawful first because the British government has been overthrown, and second because the confederation of the states has been subverted—to the lawful standing of nationhood. All the *herein*'s and *whereas*'s and *thereof*'s are not only legalisms; they also happen to be the diction of the British Empire, the language of the deposed. Nothing has changed that much, the Constitution says, lying; we are nothing that you won't recognize.

But there is something more. The key verb of the text is *shall*, as in "All legislative powers herein granted shall be vested in a Congress of the United States which shall consist of a Senate and a House of Representatives," or "New States may be admitted by the Congress into this Union; but no new State shall be formed or erected within the jurisdiction of any other State." The Constitution does not explicitly concern itself with the grievances that brought it about. It is syntactically futuristic: it prescribes what is to come. It prophesies. Even today, living 200 years into the prophecy, we read it and find it still ahead of us, still extending itself in time. The Constitution gives law and assumes for itself the power endlessly to give law. It ordains. In its articles and sections, one after another, it offers a ladder to heaven. It is cold, distant, remote as a voice from on high, self-authenticating.

Through most of history kings and their servitor churches did the ordaining, and always in the name of God. But here the people do it: "We the People . . . do ordain and establish this Constitution for the United States." And the word for God appears nowhere in the text. Heaven forbid! In fact, its very last stricture is that "no religious test shall ever be required as a qualification to any office or public trust under the United States."

The voice of the Constitution is the inescapably solemn self-consciousness of the people giving the law unto themselves. But since in the Judeo-Christian world of Western civilization all given law imitates God—God being the ultimate lawgiver—in affecting the transhuman voice of law, that dry monotone that disdains persuasion, the Constitution not only takes on the respectable sound of British statute, it more radically assumes the character of scripture.

The ordaining voice of the Constitution is scriptural, but in resolutely keeping the authority for its dominion in the public consent, it presents itself as the sacred text of secular humanism.

I wish Mrs. Brundage had told me that back in Wade Junior High School.

I wish Jerry Falwell's and Jimmy Swaggart's and Pat Robertson's teachers had taught them that back in their junior high schools.

THE SACRED TEXT

Now, it is characteristic of any sacred text that it has beyond its literal instruction tremendous symbolic meaning for the people who live by it. Think of the Torah, the Koran, the Gospels. The sacred text dispenses not just social order but spiritual identity. And as the states each in its turn ratified the Constitution, usually not without vehement debate and wrangling, the public turned out in the streets of major cities for processions, festivities, with a fresh new sense of themselves and their future.

Every major city had its ship of state rolling through the streets, pulled by teams of horses—a carpentered ship on wheels rolling around the corners and down the avenues in full sail, and perhaps with a crew of boys in sailor uniforms. It was called, inevitably, The Constitution or Federalism or Union. Companies of militia would precede it, the music of fifes and drums surround it, and children run after it, laughing at the surreal delight.

Of all the ratification processions, Philadelphia's was the grandest. There was not only a ship of state, the Union, but a float in the shape of a great eagle, drawn by six horses bearing a representation of the Constitution framed and fixed on a staff, crowned with the cap of Liberty, the words THE PEOPLE in gold letters on the staff. Even more elaborate was a slow-rolling majestic float called the New Roof, the Constitution being seen, in this case, as a structure under which society took secure shelter. The New Roof of the Constitution stood on a carriage drawn by ten white horses. Ornamented with stars, the dome was supported by thirteen pillars, each representing a state; at the top of the dome was a handsome cupola surmounted by a figure of Plenty, bearing her cornucopia. If you like the quaint charm of that, I remind you that today we speak of the framers of the Constitution, not the writers, which is more exact and realistic and less mythologically adequate.

Behind the New Roof came 450 architects, house carpenters, saw makers and file cutters, just to let people know there was now a roof-building industry available for everyone.

A thirty-foot-long float displayed a carding machine, a spinning machine of 80 spindles, a lace loom and a textile printer. There were military units in this procession, companies of light infantry and cavalry, and there were clergymen of every denomination. There were city officials and schools in their entire enrollments, but more prominent were the members of various trades, each dressed in its working clothes and carrying some display or pulling some float in advertisement of itself—sail makers and ship chandlers, cordwainers, coach builders, sign painters, clock- and watchmakers, fringe and ribbon weavers, bricklayers, tailors, spinning-wheel makers, carvers and gilders, coopers, blacksmiths, potters, wheelwrights, tinplate workers, hatters, skinners, breeches makers, gunsmiths, saddlers, stone-cutters, bakers, brewers, barber-surgeons, butchers, tanners, curriers and, I am pleased to say, printers, booksellers and stationers.

So heavily weighted was the great Philadelphia procession with those tradesmen and artisans, it could just as easily have been a labor day parade. The newly self-determined America was showing its strength and pride as a republic of hard work, in contrast to the European domains of privilege and title and their attendant poverty system. The Constitution was America de-Europeanizing itself. A kind of fission was taking place, and now here was a working-class republic, carried on the backs first of its citizen-soldiers dressed in rough brown and sober black, and then on the shoulders of its artisans and skilled workers. That anyway was the symbolic idea, the mythology that almost immediately attached itself to the ratified Constitution. From the very beginning it took on a symbolic character that its writers, worried always that they might never get it ratified, could not have foreseen. We speak of the "miracle at Philadelphia." That same impulse was working then: the celebration of the sacred text, miracles being beyond mere human understanding, a cause for wonder and gratitude— in a word, supernatural.

THE SUBTEXT

Yet it is true also of sacred texts that when they create a spiritual community, they at the same time create a larger community of the excluded. The Philistines are excluded or the pagans or the unwashed.

Even as the Constitution was establishing its sacred self in the general mind, it was still the work, the composition, of writers; and the writers were largely patrician, not working class. They tended to be well educated, wealthy and not without self-interest. The historian Carl Degler says in *Out of Our Past*: "No new social class came to power through the doors of the American Revolution. The men who engineered the revolt were largely members of the colonial ruling class." That holds for the Philadelphia 55. They themselves were aware of the benefits, if not to themselves then to their class, of the provision guaranteeing the debts incurred under the Confederation: the security holders, the creditors of America, stood to make a lot of money; at the same time, the debtors—the free holders, the small farmers—stood to lose everything. It was a practical document in their minds. They did not think of themselves as founding fathers or framers or anything more august than a group of men who held natural stewardship of the public welfare by virtue of their experience and background. They were concerned to establish a free and independent nation, but also a national economic order that would allow them to conduct business peaceably, profitably and in the stable circumstances deriving from a strong central government.

The ideals of political democracy do not always accord with the successful conduct of business. Thus, as conceived in 1787 only the House of Representatives would be elected by popular vote. Senators were to be elected by state legislatures, and the President by an electoral college, meaning men like themselves who would command the votes of their localities. There was the sense in these strictures of a need for checks and balances against popular majorities. Furthermore, to come up with a piece of paper that diverse regional business interests could agree on meant cutting deals. One such deal was between the Northeastern states and the Southern. Importation of slaves would be allowed for twenty more years; in return only a simple majority in Congress would be required to pass navigational commerce acts that the sea-going Atlantic states much wanted. That odious deal appears, in part, in Article Four of the original Constitution. The exactness and precision of statute language in this case is used not to clarify but to euphemize a practice recognizably abhorrent to the writers:

> No person held to service or labour in one State under the laws thereof, escaping into another, shall, in consequence of any law or regulation therein, be discharged from such service or labour, but shall be delivered up on claim of the party to whom such service or labour may be due.

There is no mention of the word *slave*, yet a slave in one state became a slave in all. The Virginia delegate, George Mason, to my mind the inadvertent hero of the convention, warned his colleagues: "As nations cannot be rewarded or punished in the next world they must in this. By an inevitable chain of causes and effects, Providence punishes national sins by national calamities." If you affect the scriptural voice, he could have been telling them, you had better aspire to enlightenment, or the power of prophecy of your speech will work against you. And so it came to pass. That odious article worked through a historic chain of cause and effect like a powder fuse, until the country blew apart 75 years later in civil war. Not until 1865, with the passage of the Thirteenth Amendment, was slavery outlawed in the

United States. And the monumental cost in lives, black and white, of that war, and the cost to the black people, the tragedy of their life in the antebellum South, and to American blacks everywhere since then (the state poll taxes that kept black people from voting in the South were not outlawed until the Twenty-fourth Amendment was ratified, in 1964), shows how potent, how malignly powerful, the futuristic, transhuman Constitution has been where it has been poorly written. What was sacred is profane; there is a kind of blasphemous inversion of the thing.

In this formulation it is the power of the Constitution to amend itself, or, in writers' terms, to accept revision, that shows the delegates at their best. They knew what they had was imperfect, a beginning; Franklin and Washington said as much. Nevertheless, Mason refused to put his name to the constitutional document even after Franklin urged a unanimous presentation to the states, because of the slavery article and also because there was no Bill of Rights—no explicit statutes on the rights of American citizens to free speech and assembly and religious practice, and to speedy trial by jury of defendants in criminal charges; no prohibition against government search and seizure without judicial warrant; no guarantee of a free press and so forth. Alexander Hamilton argued that those things were implicit in the Constitution and did not have to be spelled out, much as people now say the Equal Rights Amendment is unnecessary, but Mason, to his credit, knew that they must be spelled out, which is to say written. Imagine where we would be today if Mason had not held his ground and if the lack of a Bill of Rights had not been taken up as the major concern of the antifederalists, such as Patrick Henry. We would be trusting our rights and liberties to the reading of the Attorney General, who today believes that people who are defendants in criminal trials are probably guilty or they would not be defendants, and who has said that the American Civil Liberties Union is essentially a criminals' lobby. George Mason's amendments, the first ten, were passed on to the states for ratification by the first elected Congress in 1791.

It is true of most of the sacred texts, I think, that a body of additional law usually works itself up around the primary material, and also achieves the force of prophecy. The Torah has its Talmud, and the Koran its *hadith*, and the New Testament its apostolic teachings. In like manner we have our sacred secular humanist amendments. Mythic or sacred time is endless, of course, and it was not until 1920, with the passage of the Nineteenth Amendment, that the women of the United States achieved suffrage. (I am told that this amendment has still not been ratified by the state of Georgia.)

HERMENEUTICS

I notice at this point a certain change of tone: my song of the miracle of Philadelphia has wobbled a bit; my voice has broken, and here I am speaking in the bitter caw of the critic. Yet there is a kind of inevitability to this. One cannot consider the Constitution of the United States without getting into an argument with it. It is the demand of the sacred text that its adherents not just believe in it but engage to understand its meanings, its values, its revelation. One finds every day in the newspapers the continuing argument with the Constitution, as different elements of society represent their versions of its truth. President Reagan argues with it, Attorney General Edwin Meese argues with it, and so, as a defenseless citizen from a different point of view, do I. And, of course, the federal judiciary has amended, interpreted and derived law from it. From the days of the great John Marshall on down—way down—to the days of William Rehnquist, the courts have not just worshiped the Constitution; they have read it. Their readings are equivalent to the priestly commentaries that accrue to every sacred text, and the commentaries on the commentaries, and we have 200 years of these as statute and opinion.

It is the nature of the sacred text, speaking from the past to the present and into the future in that scriptural voice that does not explain, embellish itself, provide the source of its ideas or the intentions from which it is written, but which is packed with wild history—the self-authenticating text that is pared of all emotions in the interest of clear and precise law-giving—it is the nature of such a text, paradoxically, to shimmer with ambiguity and to become finally enigmatic, as if it were the ultimate voice of Buddhist self-realization.

And so I find here in my reflections a recapitulation of the debate of American constitutional studies of the past 200 years, in the same manner that ontogeny recapitulates phylogeny. Thus it was in the nineteenth century that historians such as George Bancroft celebrated the revolutionary nature of the Founding Fathers' work, praising them for having conceived of a republic of equal rights under law, constructed from the materials of the European Enlightenment but according to their own pragmatic Yankee design—a federalism of checks and balances that would withstand the worst buffetings of history, namely the Civil War, in the aftermath of which Bancroft happened to be writing.

Then in the early part of the twentieth century, when the worst excesses of American business were coming to light, one historian, Charles Beard, looked at old Treasury records and other documents and discovered enough to assert that the Fathers stood to gain personally from the way they put the thing together, at least their class did; that they were mostly wealthy men and lawyers; and that the celebrated system of checks and balances, rather than insuring a distribution of power and a democratic form of government, in fact could be seen as having been devised to control populist sentiment and prevent a true majoritarian politics from operating in American life at the expense of property rights. Madison had said as much, Beard claimed, in *Federalist* number 10, which he wrote to urge ratification. Beard's economic interpretation of the Constitution has ever since governed scholarly debate. At the end of the Depression a neo-Beardian, Merrill Jensen, looked again at the post-Revolutionary period and came up with a thesis defending the Articles of Confederation as the true legal instrument of the Revolution, which, with modest amendments, could have effected the peace and order of the states with more democracy than a centralist government. In fact, he argued, there was no crisis under the Articles or danger of anarchy, except in the minds of the wealthy men who met in Philadelphia.

But countervailing studies appeared in the 1950s, the era of postwar conservatism, that showed Beard's research to be inadequate, asserting, for instance, that there were as many wealthy men of the framers' class who were against ratification as who were for it, or that men of power and influence tended to react according to the specific needs of their own states and localities, coastal or rural, rather than according to class.

And in the 1960s, the Kennedy years, a new argument appeared describing the Constitutional Convention above all as an exercise of democratic politics, a nationalist reform caucus that was genuinely patriotic, improvisational and always aware that what it did must win popular approval if it was to become the law of the land.

In my citizen's self-instruction I embrace all of those interpretations. I believe all of them. I agree that something unprecedented and noble was created in Philadelphia; but that economic class self-interest was a large part of it; but that it was democratic and improvisational; but that it was, at the same time, something of a coup. I think all of those theories are true, simultaneously.

THE 200TH YEAR

And what of constitutional scholarship today, in the Age of Reagan?

Well, my emphasis on text, my use of textual analogy, responds to the work over the past few years of a new generation of legal scholars who have been arguing among themselves as to whether the Constitution can be seen usefully as a kind of literary text, sustaining intense interpretive reading—as a great poem, say—or better perhaps as a form of scripture. I have swiveled to embrace both of those critiques too, but adding, as a professional writer, that when I see the other professions become as obsessively attentive to text as mine is, I suspect it is a sign that we live in an age in which the meanings of words are dissolving, in which the culture of discourse itself seems threatened. That is my view of America under Reagan today: in literary critical terms, I would describe his administration as deconstructionist.

And so, by way of preservation, text consciousness may have arisen among us, law professors no less than novelists, as in medieval times monks began painstakingly copying the crumbling parchments to preserve them.

All told, it is as if the enigmatic constitutional text cannot be seen through, but, shimmering in ambiguity, dazzles back at each generation in its own times and struggles. It is as if the ambiguity is not in the text but in us, as we struggle in our natures—our consciences with our appetites, our sense of justice with our animal fears and self-interests—just as the Founding Fathers struggled so with their Constitution, providing us with a mirror of ourselves to go on shining, shining back at us through the ages, as the circumstances of our lives change, our costumes change, our general store is transformed into a mile-long twenty-four-hour shopping mall, our trundle carts transmogrify into rockets in space, our country paves over, and our young republic becomes a plated armory of ideological warfare: a mirror for us to see who we are and who we would like to be, the sponsors of private armies of thugs and rapists and murderers, or the last best hope of mankind.

It may be that as a result of World War II and the past forty years of our history we are on the verge, as a nation, of some characterological change that neither the federalists of the convention nor the antifederalists who opposed them could have foreseen or endorsed. We are evolving under *Realpolitik* circumstances into a national military state—with a militarized economy larger than, and growing at the expense of, a consumer economy; a militarized scientific-intellectual establishment; and a bureaucracy of secret paramilitary intelligence agencies—that becomes increasingly self-governing and unlegislated. There may be no news in any of this. What may be news, however, is the extent to which the present administration has articulated a rationale for this state of being, so that culture too, both secular and religious, can be seen as beginning to conform to the needs of a national security state. More than any previous administration this one apotheosizes not law but a carelessness or even contempt of law, as internationally it scorns the World Court and domestically it refuses to enforce federal civil rights statutes or honor the decrees of judicial review, or gives into private hands the conduct of foreign policy outlawed by the Congress. And more than any previous administration this one discourses not in reason and argument but in demagogic pieties. Its lack of reverence for law and contempt for language seem to go hand in hand.

By contrast, I call your attention to the great genius of the convention of 1787, which was its community of discourse. The law it designed found character from the means of its designing. Something arose from its deliberations, however contentious, and that was the empowering act of composition given to people who know what words mean and how they must be valued. Nobody told anybody else to love it or leave it; nobody told anybody else to go back where they came from; nobody suggested disagreement was disloyalty; and nobody pulled a gun. Ideas, difficult ideas, were articulated with language and disputed with language and took their final fate, to be passed or rejected, as language. The possibility of man-made law with the authority, the moral imperative, of God's law, inhered in the process of making it.

That is what we celebrate as citizens today. That is what we cherish and honor, a document that gives us the means by which we may fearlessly argue ourselves into clarity as a free and unified people. To me the miracle at Philadelphia was finally the idea of democratic polity, a foot in the door of the new house for all man and womankind. The relentless logic of a Constitution in the name of the people is that a national state exists for their sake, not the other way around. The undeviating logic of a Constitution in the name of the people is that the privilege of life under its domain is equitable, which is to say, universal. That you cannot have democracy only for yourself or your club or your class or your church or your clan or your color or your sex, for then the word doesn't mean what it says. That once you write the prophetic text for a true democracy—as our forefathers did in their draft and as our amending legislators and judiciary have continued to do in their editing of its moral self-contradictions and methodological inadequacies—that once this text is in voice, it cannot be said to be realized on earth until all the relations among the American people, legal relations, property relations, are made just.

And I reflect now, in conclusion, that this is what brought the people into the streets in Philadelphia 200 years ago, those wheelwrights and coach builders and ribbon and fringe weavers: the idea, the belief, the faith that America was unprecedented.

I'd like to think, in this year of the bicentennial celebration, that the prevailing image will be of those plain people taking to the streets, people with only their wit and their skills to lead them through their lives, forming their processions: the wheelwrights and ribbon makers, the railroad porters and coal miners, the garment workers, the steelworkers, the automobile workers, the telephone operators, the air traffic controllers, the farm workers, the computer programmers and, one hopes, the printers, stationers and booksellers too.

. . .

A CITIZEN'S READING

A good annotated constitutional text at the secondary-school level is *Your Rugged Constitution*, by Bruce and Esther Findlay (Stanford University Press, 1952). Of the available dramatic reconstructions of the Constitutional Convention of 1787, I relied most heavily on *The Great Rehearsal*, by Carl Van Doren (Viking, 1948). All popular studies of the convention depend on the original scholarship of Max Farrand, whose *The Framing of the Constitution of the United States* (Yale University Press, 1913) is a classic contribution.

My view of the sociopolitical ferment in America before and after the Revolution owes much to Howard Zinn's *A People's History of the United States* (Harper & Row, 1980), a bracing antidote to complacent historiography, and to *The Americans*, by J. C. Furnas (G.P. Putnam's Sons, 1969), a compendious examination of daily life from the Colonial period to the twentieth century. My summary of the scholarly debate from Bancroft and Beard on through the 1960s would have been difficult without *Essays on the Making of the Constitution*, edited by Leonard W. Levy (Oxford University Press, 1969). This astute anthology presents the central ideas of the major constitutional historians in excerpt, thus relieving the lay person of the necessity of reading their important works in entirety.

Finally, although the following scholars may take exception to the uses I've made of their work, I credit my conversion to constitutional scripturalism to James Boyd White, "The Judicial Opinion and the Poem: Ways of Reading, Ways of Life" (*Michigan Law Review*, Vol. 82:1669, 1984), and "Law as Language: Reading Law and Reading Literature" (*Texas Law Review*, Vol. 60:415, 1982); Thomas C. Grey, "The Constitution as Scripture" (*Stanford Law Review*, Vol. 37:1, 1984); and Sanford Levinson, "The Constitution in American Civil Religion" (*Supreme Court Review*, 1979).

E. L. DOCTOROW

Many readers have enjoyed the superb fiction of E. L. Doctorow. We think that not as many are as aware of his brilliant essays, which are so remarkably original.

In 1986 he was asked to speak about the U.S. Constitution at Independence Hall in Philadelphia. The Pennsylvania Humanities Council was arranging the celebration of a centennial.

The essay Doctorow produced is as much an analysis of the text of the great document (and the manner of its interpretations) as it is a study of the framers, the human beings who sat in Philadelphia creating a new country.

Doctorow reads the framers and their work with the intense eye of the novelist. We come away knowing the central document of American life better than ever before—perhaps like this for the first time.

E. L. Doctorow has published the novels Big As Life, Welcome to Hard Times, The Book of Daniel, Ragtime, Loon Lake, World's Fair, *and* Billy Bathgate. *He has also published a collection of short fiction,* Lives of the Poets, *and a play,* Drinks Before Dinner, *originally produced at the Public Theatre in New York City.*

TESTIMONIES

TESTIMONIES

Catherine Gammon

THE END

SHE DIED IN A PLANE CRASH. SHE'D GIVEN HIS LANDLORD A HUNDRED-dollar deposit on the apartment next door, then gone west to visit her mother. On the way back, the plane came down. Murphy'd already left the Bronx for Dallas and it was only later that George gave him the news (Murphy calling deep in winter, asking, well, how were they all? then remembering he too had flown at about that time and thanking his lucky stars it wasn't him—his thanks a little wishful, almost a prayer, underneath it, God, a bright clear bourbon drunk, Why not me? Why not me?).

George had often imagined her dying. She would have said it was in his nature to project anything vital into a state of fatal decay, would have labeled it his pessimism, morbidity. He denies this, calls it realism—she smoked two packs a day. He dreamed her stupefied at forty, nothing remaining but cancer of the lungs. When she'd said she was going west, he'd never doubted her return. He only dreamed crashes when it was he who was to fly. It was not her logical death—there was nothing in her life to suggest such a dying. She was too young. Forty would have been too young. She had the kind of spirit that would still be young at eighty. Why kill it? He'd pressured her to quit. Even during the weeks when he was smoking, too—in the dead of winter, in early spring—he raised the specter of disease. Had he been at all like Murphy he'd have quit once only. Nobody would guess he'd ever smoked. He wouldn't handle unlit cigarettes with tender craving, wouldn't carry toothpicks to suck between his lips, wouldn't conjure images of loved friends dying or see himself an old man and lone survivor still lusting for a drag.

But he was not like Murphy. He was all on the surface, all outside. One of the things they had in common, he and she. Visibility.

One of the things they'd had in common.

Thirty-two. Dead. Unfinished. Terminated. Mid-sentence, no doubt. Wearing red probably. Smoking. Drinking a Jack Daniel's. Eager to arrive. To move in next door. To begin the second fall, to enter winter.

Useless. Useless, George.

He drank a solid month, smoked packs. There she was, night after night, bright, alive, talking fast to strangers in the air, sitting quiet, staring out the window. Here she was, leaning across a table in a bar, walking silent streets untouching at his side, haunting the empty rooms—waving cigarettes, always waving cigarettes.

There was no one he could mourn to openly and fully. Not even Murphy. Murphy didn't know half. Let him find out somewhere else. A few words on the phone and who knew if he'd ever stop crying?

When it got so bad that he began to imagine it was not the malfunction of the DC-10 that killed her but his own unspoken hopes (hopes that for sanity's sake he'd had to deny), George suddenly pulled himself together. He quit smoking once again, quit drinking. An unemployed actress moved into the next apartment. The same old story. Scar tissue forms. Life goes on.

THE STAND-IN

His was one of those names. If you're Jim or Bill or John you have one of those names. Everyone called him Murphy. Even women, making love. "Oh. Oh, Murphy. Murphy, oh, Murphy Murphy Murphy!" Except when they forgot themselves, in ecstasy misplaced him, named him Richard, David, Fred, or Joe. It hadn't happened often. Often enough, though—more often than to most. It was because they knew. Yes, he thought. The best of them knew. He didn't want relationships with women. Just the women. He liked them. They made good friends, better than men. More reliable. More careful not to offend. They talked. They were generous. They laughed, with and at him. They seemed to understand. He encouraged them. What he did not want was this thing they called relationship. He actually enjoyed the lapses when the names got crossed. A woman with a man of her own was his best protection against disaster. Only once had the strategy led him into his own trap. Mea culpa, Murphy muttered, mea culpa. Goodbye, Marie, goodbye. It took forever to disentangle himself. She'd left her husband, claiming it wasn't because of *him*. But Murphy knew. For a month or two they were happy, then it was three years of downhill slide. All the way to Texas to get free. He still saw her from time to time. He wouldn't say he didn't love her. He did. But it—that thing—that false identity . . . no thank you, friends. He'd loved her best when she belonged to someone else.

THE OBLIGATORY BLOND

Let the record show that we are all blonds. In varying degree. It might be said that I am the blondest. There were also brunettes involved, but among the women, they were marginal. Which is to say, committed.

What Murphy and I have in common is our Catholicism. I'm a blond Italian Catholic from New Orleans. He's a black-haired Irish Catholic from the Bronx. No matter. We were born in the same year. We've never been lovers, and never will be. I was meant to be a nun, he a priest. The rest bear no such burden—all WASPs. It's Murphy and I who live in constant knowledge of vocation denied. Elizabeth, George, Maude all had some kind of conscience, Jack pretends to have none, but whatever its character—honest or dishonest, flexible or rigid, deceiving or deceived—conscience is always solitary: self-contained and individual. Of that isolation Murphy and I are free. In spirit if not in fact we still commune with millions—we dwell with them in guilt. In our hearts we are virgin. We wallow in original sin. My essence is little girl.

Even Elizabeth never understood this. She saw my difficulties as tasks heroically to be mastered. She aimed for wisdom. The function of her conscience was to guide her—to lead her into action, through knowledge, on the path of her own rightness, to perfection. (I don't want you to get the wrong idea—what she saw as right was not always what the world would see, but she trusted her instinct and analysis to clarify what was right or wrong for her. When she lost that clarity, she was as confused as anyone else.) Guilt she did not understand—guilt, for her, was a warning only, a sign. Like an ache in the belly that said some organ was misfunctioning, guilt was an instruction that some act committed was in error, not to be repeated. Message received, lesson learned. Thank you, guilt, goodbye. She did not understand guilt as a state, a gift, an innocence—to be preserved.

I have only recently realized what a danger Elizabeth was to this preservation. She saw too well. Saw things before they happened. Not in any psychic way. Nothing occult. She just knew. Mental. A chronicler of minute changes, she was the sort of woman who, when younger, was too often told that she thought too much. Her interpretations implied predictions the accuracy of which amazes me only in retrospect. I had come to rely on her analyses and intuitions to understand everything that went on around us. There's confusion out there now—at the same time, I am no longer threatened, I no longer hear her voice crying *Grow up, Renee* beneath her words.

I give you this as an example: It was she who made me aware of Jack as a man who desired me. Until that night he had lived for me in imagination only, pure and unattainable. We had all eaten dinner together, at Elizabeth's. She wanted cigarettes. Outside it was cold, bitter, wet. Jack wanted to go dancing. No one else felt like moving. I said I'd go for the cigarettes. Jack and I walked. I bought the cigarettes and came back. Jack came back with me, sullen. Elizabeth was stunned to see us. "You didn't go dancing?" she demanded. I didn't know what I'd misunderstood. In the kitchen she explained. I felt like a dunce. Or that she was crazy. Still, I went to him. She wasn't crazy. I refused him that night but not before he'd shown me what Elizabeth had already seen. It made me giddy. Things wakened in me that before had slept. I'd never had a fantasy lover turn real. If Elizabeth hadn't spoken, if she hadn't read desire in his gestures of that night, our affair would never have begun, he would still be a perfect prince in my private dream world, not the bastard male like all the others he finally is. Without Elizabeth, his desire would have slipped right by me, as things slip by me now. Maybe I'm better off. I no longer have Elizabeth insisting, while I obsess and suffer, that if I want what I get from him I have to be willing to pay the price, I have to grow up, Renee, grow up.

In the end she didn't like me. Because I rejected her knowledge. She would never have said that, don't get me wrong. But I felt it. For herself she regarded sex as exploration, expansion of the mind. To know and to be known. That's not accurate either. She loved her body. Start there. But she also loved what a man's body could give her of the man—through her body to her mind. She was very intricate, was Elizabeth. There were things the mind could learn through the body that it could learn no other way. And if one put the body into the fire one had to be willing to burn. It was part of the knowledge of fire. It took a lifetime to master the balances. Coming unhinged was welcome—the sign of something new. She saw my troubles as if from a great height, as if she had known them far in her past. There were only four years between us but they might have been four centuries. I valued her wisdom. But I didn't want it. I don't believe she valued my simplicity. Perhaps it isn't the proper thing to say, but in all honesty I'm sure I must be safer now she's gone.

THINGS THEY
HAD IN COMMON

Both of their fathers had died the summer before they met. Each was an only child. Also: blue eyes; three centuries of American ancestry; integrity apparent in all matters but those of sex; borderline alcoholism; love and pain; tenderness; hysteria of the kind that has learned to laugh at itself without relinquishing its suffering; generosity of spirit; breadth of understanding; depth of heart. They loved frequently and long.

IN WINTER

Murphy had to laugh. It was the slowest seduction he'd ever witnessed. It had been going on for months even before he'd come back to town. The night he first met her, George took him by and she gave them wine. He could see they shared a secret. He was astonished when George told him later the secret never was. It was peculiar to see him in a state of doubt about a woman. "You're getting old," Murphy teased. When he'd last lived here, George was complexly involved with Maude and still with some woman who'd long since left for Philadelphia—not to mention his wife (estranged but not abandoned) and half a dozen other women waiting in lofts and basement apartments, anxious to wish him good will, good luck, goodbye. This year George was forty.

Occasionally Murphy imagined George was trying to mix him up with Elizabeth, introducing him as an obstacle to his own desire. Murphy considered it—she might be safe, a romp, a fling, no complications. Her passion was clearly for George. But he couldn't be sure. His interest wasn't strong enough to overcome the hesitation. Too often the way with him. Girls he met in disco bars were so much easier. Like his students back in Dallas. They looked up to him. Any trouble they might give him would be limited by their awe. Elizabeth lacked awe. She treated him like an equal— casual, indifferent. She was older. Not that he didn't like her, he rather did. But he was quick to sense danger. He recognized that her reserve in relation to George was not temperamental but circumstantial—dictated perhaps by Maude. Let George do it, he thought. Play with fire. Go up in smoke.

He was amazed the night they finally brought it off. The three of them had been drinking till they ran out of cash. George offered steak and eggs. Murphy headed home for beer and his car, George and Elizabeth headed for George's.

When he joined them there—her shoes off, their shirts half unbuttoned, George flushed—Murphy had to laugh. They might have been teenagers interrupted by someone's mother. It was only then he believed what George had been implying: he'd never touched her.

George cooked. Elizabeth sat at the table, opening bottles. Murphy watched her. He'd never really understood the fascination. Suddenly he did. She glowed. How had George seen it? Murphy sighed. He knew he'd seen it himself but had given it another name.

When the knock came they were sitting around the table, eating, laughing at nothing. Murphy being closest reached behind his chair to unlatch the door. Oh no, he howled, silent. Jennifer, the girl downstairs. "I saw your light," she told George. Murphy smirked. When he finally said he had to leave, Elizabeth glanced at him, panic all over her face, then to her lover. George reached across the table and touched her arm. "It's all right," Murphy either heard

or imagined. Instantly she glowed again. Murphy laughed
all the way home.

THINGS APART

He preferred Tolstoy, she Dostoevsky. Also: hair color (his
brown, hers blond); families (his never left New England,
hers roamed west); guilt (his physical, hers intellectual);
guilts (outwardly he let them go, they consumed him from
within—she, vice versa); cigarettes (he always quit, she
refused to); pain and love; anger (his stubborn but modest,
hers intemperate but short-lived); humors (hers from sor-
row, his from pity); economics (he was rich, living below his
means—she was poor, living above them); labors (he was
unemployed and made art, she worked and made the rent);
breadth of heart (his wide, hers narrow); depth of understanding (his slow to penetrate, hers immediate to the core).
Old lovers lingered in his life, hers in memory. She loved
serially, he multiply. She was single, he was not.

ANOTHER BLOND

What can I say about Maude? I never really knew her. She
had a great wide smile, as did Elizabeth. In other ways they
were similar: in coloring and build, practical intelligence,
force of purpose. In singularity.

Maude was always laughing. Elizabeth also laughed,
but differently. While Maude's laugh was giddy, Elizabeth's
was rhetorical, used specifically to undermine the spoken
word. What they shared was mobility of feature. Expres-
siveness. Speed of change. My own face I know to be
masklike, flat, fixed—an icon. Not theirs. Their bodies were

fluid, like their faces. Unconscious but always aware. It's odd they didn't know each other better. Perhaps they didn't need to.

Elizabeth was aware of the similarities. Also of their difference. "Maude lives in the world," she told me, "you live in the mind—I walk a tightrope strung between the two." Then she laughed. Always striving for connection, she suffered from vertigo. Sometimes no one could decipher her messages but herself. When she was younger she'd been puzzled when her clarity of insight left listeners confused. By the time we knew her, she'd learned. She laughed after she spoke, tossed her head, retreated into her hair. She poured another drink. The irony was never in her words, in her mind, but she would give us a gesture from which to infer it. She turned a formal phrase in order to destroy it with a mocking tone of voice. It was learned behavior. She was no longer accused of taking herself too seriously. She still did.

She differed from me in this: she was driven to reveal. Had she kept her mental life to herself, these elaborate stratagems surrounding its presence in the world would not have been necessary. I hide. It's easier.

As for Maude, there are facts. She was married, but lived apart from her husband. He was in graduate school, somewhere south. Jack once said of him—enviously, mystified—that he didn't have a jealous bone in his body. There'd been a time when she was openly living with George, the husband temporarily forgotten. This was before I knew them. A last word about her: she, like many of us, was to leave in the summer, but unlike most of us, she wasn't coming back. Her husband, having completed his Ph.D., would be teaching in Boston. She planned to join him there.

MISERIES

The fact was he did not have room in his life for Elizabeth. He simply wanted her. He'd barely got everything straight with Maude when she arrived. He was afraid. He'd held off for months, but when Murphy turned away that night to fetch the beer, he knew their hour had come. "I have dreams about you," he told her, mocking himself, sadly, confused. He didn't believe in dreams. "I know," she said, "me too." She laughed. "We walk around the streets together, never touching." After they spent that night together, the dreams were laid to rest. Then came a Saturday noon a month later when he ran into her and Murphy coming down Murphy's stairs. They said hello, they were off to breakfast. George drank the rest of the day and found himself at midnight— some god knew how, not George—with them, all silent, Murphy wry, George waiting for him to leave. Elizabeth wanted pizza. Murphy was willing. It sounded like a code. Don't be hungry, Elizabeth, let him go. But they walked, the three of them. Murphy urged him to join them, to eat. He wouldn't. He was heading home. She stared straight forward, lingering at his side while Murphy led. "All right then," George whispered, "if this is what you want. But watch out for yourself. Be careful." She gave no sign of hearing. Murphy urged him again. He refused and waved them goodnight. The dreams returned.

MURPHY'S LAW

Whatever can go wrong, will.

During all that winter, that spring, I was involved in my own obsessive clandestine relations with Jack. That moment's intersection between her affairs and mine had brought Elizabeth and me together as unnatural confidantes. Our intimacy grew and with it my feeling that she didn't like me. Only too late have I understood that it wasn't me she disliked. She needed me, a witness, couldn't live without revelation, yet as she spoke, the hard, clear, magnifying lens that was her conscience projected that endless lucidity onto me. She didn't hear her words, she saw them in my face, until it disappeared behind the negative of her own.

Without me to serve this function, of course, she would have had to seek out someone else. How much simpler it is—and kinder—to remain as a child, only pretending to adulthood, quietly and innocently enjoying one's sins, acknowledging them as sin only to the future, before God, where all life will, in any case, be sinful. These people called it wisdom to fuss about this world. I call it folly. Consider Elizabeth. She was cursed by her competence. Whatever she took up she could do. In the country of the blind the one-eyed man is king. That was Elizabeth. There was always someone after her, demanding her skills, her flexibility, her mind. Overworked and underpaid. Because with her competence came a dread. She must keep her conscience clean. Only those who can bear to be guilty are capable of accepting large responsibilities. Thus she was always meagerly employed. She rejected any job that required her soul—as any intelligent job must, except when given to one who knows disguise.

Elizabeth put no pressure on George. When she was younger she'd believed that passion alone determined right—passion being true, truth being the only condition opposed to error. Older, she'd changed. Passion must wait its time. She even started things with Murphy just because he was free. After she spent that night with him she spoke of being spellbound "in the body only—it's all in the mind." Does this make sense? Not to me. She made some fine distinction between real and false desire. George represented real desire, Murphy false. Oh, there were other reasons besides Murphy's freedom—he was attractive, certainly. They had a witty, ironical sort of friendship. They shared an interest in Kierkegaard. But none of this was essential. What mattered was her sure recognition that with Murphy there would be no wounded other woman whose ghost she must violate by living: her conscience would be still.

It happened almost inconspicuously. A late-night crowd had gathered at Murphy's to devour chili and beer. Elizabeth never left. She told me later she'd known all along they would have that night. Nothing obvious was said or done, there was no plan, almost no intention—just the recognition that they would take that night. But then she grew uneasy. Vaguely spellbound in the body (afterlust, she called it) but mentally clear, she knew there was no certainty that Murphy would have any further desire for her. She wasn't sure he'd really desired her at all. It's why she called it false. (I'm trying to reconstruct her way of thinking that week. None of it made enough sense to me. The distinctions are too subtle, too fine for their subject, which is after all more basic and less complex than a mind like Elizabeth's allowed.) She had no certainty, either, of her own desire for him. She imagined that if he acted she would respond, but she cared not enough to act on her own behalf. And there had been the warnings. Jack told me offhandedly that Murphy had a history of cruelty to women. I wasn't sure if he meant this for me or for Elizabeth but I passed it on. She said she'd heard something similar from another source. She was cautious. She would not be humiliated, would not give the slightest gesture that could indicate either expectation or intention and leave her wide open for insult if cruelty were in fact Murphy's way. She said he couldn't hurt her, he didn't mean enough to her to hurt her. She made it clear she had no fear of humiliation itself—that when desire was strong, when she was sure, then risks were worth the taking. But not in a case like this, she insisted—a case that existed only in the mind.

Frankly, I thought she was kidding herself, pretending only, in case Murphy proved really to be indifferent. I'd never understood what she saw in George. Murphy was without question the more attractive. As it turned out, though, I misjudged her feelings. I learned it when I meddled by giving a dinner, thinking she and Murphy needed a nudge. When she arrived (late) I got the impression my plan was going to work. She was unusually radiant. Instantly they were teasing each other. It seemed they were agreed again, as they had so mysteriously been agreed before. Several hours later we all left my place to go dancing. No sooner had we arrived than she walked straight up to George, who was standing alone at the bar. She never left him. They slipped away together as neatly as if the meeting had been prearranged. It wasn't.

MORE MURPHY'S LAW

Murphy turned around from the bar and searched the tables, the dance floor. Whatever can go wrong, he thought, must. They were gone. For a week he'd hesitated. Over pizza that night he'd set the right tone (telling her stories of his Texas college girls, getting her laughing at the horror the sophomore had shown when he'd asked, "Do you want to eat first?"—"First?" she cried—and his own horror at having brought home a virgin who proceeded to imagine he was secretly in love with her because he drove her to the dorm so promptly once he knew). At his stairs he'd said, "Good night," clear and firm. "I'll see you tomorrow," specific stress on the tomorrow. He'd let her walk on home alone. It would not have done to have her back so soon. No two nights in succession. Basic rule. But he had not run into her tomorrow, or sought her out. He didn't know why. Caution, he told himself. They went to lunch a day later. There was an afternoon walk on the beach. They did laundry together one evening. Nothing came of it. It must have been a week before they walked home again (from a party, another bar night, who could remember?) and she paused automatically at his stairs to say good night. He said she was too drunk to manage alone and grabbed her by the elbow to pull her up the street. She laughed, then said, "I feel peculiar about sleeping with you the other night."

"Tell the whole world," he muttered. "I don't."

What did she mean? What did he mean? At her door he waited to see what would come. She looked at him like a monkey. Did he want her or didn't he? She never looked at George that way. Why? It wasn't necessary. With him she believed in what she did. Now she was acting. She was a bad actress. Murphy smirked.

"Well," she said, touching his elbows. He gave her a quick kiss.

"Oh, so cool," she said.

That's better, he thought. That's Elizabeth. "Then quit making monkey faces at me."

"Monkey faces!" She flared and vanished before he could stop her.

When he saw her on the street and mentioned Renee's invitation, she was funny. She was invited too. Had she known he was coming or hadn't she? Was it a scheme? The very possibility of such a question bored him. But he'd enjoyed her. And she was a puzzle. He wasn't quite sure how things had become so difficult. They'd driven to the beach that day, walked in the sand. It was then something might have been said, done. He'd expected her to speak. Women always spoke. They asked to have the terms defined. As if one were making contracts. But nothing happened. He was anxious then about the dinner. He wondered if he might be walking into some kind of trap. He was relieved to find several other guests there when he arrived. That Elizabeth was late was unusual. She was habitually punctual, often early. She got involved in a book she said when she finally showed up, lost track of time. He warmed to her. She seemed easy again at last. As if his cool kiss, his accusation of monkey faces, had cleared the air between them. By the time they left Renee's, he found himself wanting to take her home. Then suddenly there she was, leaning into George. And that was that.

What had been lacking, he decided, was a leap of faith. Though two leaps were ideal, action required only one. Much as he believed in the leap when it came to existential, theological philosophy, it was—after all—essential paradox, hardly suited (for his own temper, at least) to application in daily life. Lucky for him that she'd already leapt. Otherwise, he thought, it might have come at him. He shuddered. He could feel her burning everything in sight.

Still, his week of uncertainty had left him restless. He was conscious of his loneliness in a way he had not been before. It's nearly spring, he told himself, it's only the season. But he grew wistful. His imagination turned to Maude.

NIGHT TERRORS

Sensation in the brain. Physical breaking. In blacklit wakefulness, tiny bursts of feeling that are not thoughts or memories, aches or pains. Just sensations. Events of a magnitude too small to be defined. They were absent (which is to say imperceptible) only if she were (as two or three times a month she was) completely drunk, or when she dropped into a sexual sleep, sharing a bed with a man. Other nights (which is to say most of her nights) they kept her watchful. Always at these moments it seemed another day could never come. To put a stop to it she resorted to silent recitation of the Twenty-third Psalm (tending to omit the paths of righteousness). She never spoke of these terrors, nor of their remedy. Who could have believed her? Both contradicted all that was knowable about her. She lay awake listening to crackles, one by one. She felt each snap in its specific location. She imagined a fragile lining at the surface of her brain—gauzelike but hard as fine crystal—serving to maintain the delicate separation between what was inside and what was out. Slowly, night after night, this thin crystalline darkness was shattering—in one minute black plosion after another. They frightened her, these infinitesimal events.

COME SPRING

On Easter Sunday he bought her a beer. He knew that not long before she'd been with George and a crowd of others at an oyster-and-bloody-Mary breakfast he'd scrupulously avoided. He was sitting with Maude in the window of the corner bar when she happened by. She joined them.

"I'm not interrupting anything?"

"Not at all, not at all, let me buy you a beer." He was up and gone before she could protest. Maude had been lamenting George. Christ on the Cross, Murphy muttered, in three weeks I can have my pick.

F L I G H T

George never flew without being certain for weeks in advance that the plane would crash. In mid-April he was leaving for North Africa. As the date drew near, he drank more heavily. He lost caution. The night before his departure he told Elizabeth what would happen to the plane. She asked if he really believed that.

"Always."

He hated to leave her. He imagined Murphy, zooming in for the kill.

E L I Z A B E T H ' S   D R E A M

Elizabeth was the first to interpret Murphy and Maude. She'd read it on Easter, she said. She told me nothing until she'd observed them further, convinced her observations were different from those made by others (Jack, for example) of Murphy and herself—she was careful nonetheless to speak in time to be oracular. When I casually suggested that after George was gone she might start up again with Murphy, she laughed, said she didn't think so, she believed he was now involved with Maude. This led to speculation. Had George ended it with Maude then? Did his imminent depar-

ture, his involvement with Elizabeth, Maude's coming re-
union with her husband—had all this separated them,
leaving Maude temporarily free? Or had George connived to
give her to Murphy simply to distract him from Elizabeth?
Let me make it clear that Elizabeth speculated none of this
aloud. I can only guess. But my guesses are stamped with
the workings of her mind. Even now it's hard to be free
of them.

One thing she did tell me that may reveal something was
a dream. She was standing at a second-story window (in an
apartment she'd once had in San Francisco) looking down. It
was night. Across the street there were lights in the windows
of a jeweler, and running in the street was a group of men
and women, twenty or so in number. Some of them were
dressed in ordinary clothes, some wore masks, capes, glit-
tery makeup, and feathers. Half swarmed in one direction,
half in another, but all were together, running and shouting,
hovering about the shop. She called them anarchists. Precisely what she meant she didn't say. She knew them for what
they were, immediately, as one does in dreams. (There are
dreams which pass unnoticed, and those which are remembered only to be forgotten, and there are those, she would
say, which never leave—which are remembered not only as
recalled in words, but as originally experienced, in the
images themselves. She said she could see the images of this
dream quite clearly by calling them up, in the same way one
can see a particular face in one's mind simply by asking for
it.) They dragged the jeweler out to the street. He was a Jew.
She knew this as she had known the anarchists. She remained at her window watching in fascination. She could see
many of their faces. They were not people she recognized.
They led the jeweler off, but some of their number lingered,
and having seen her watching, crossed in her direction. It

occurred to her she should be afraid, but she wasn't. She had the distinct thought: I'm on their side. She knew, she thought, what they wanted with the jeweler. (It all had to do with the Palestinians, she said. I didn't ask her what.) "I am on your side," she told them. Three men or four climbed the fire escape to her window, which had acquired a balcony. They hung there, staring. "We're only taking him to a meeting, to show him a film. He won't be hurt. We want him to understand. Next week we'll come for you."

"I'm on your side," she said again.

The man who had spoken laughed. "Next week we want you."

"I may not be free."

"We want *you*," he said, "Elizabeth. Next week at seven-thirty."

They left her. She walked back from the window into her room. Suddenly she realized she was wearing the black lace underpants I'd given her for her birthday the week before. She wanted to see herself in a mirror. Not wanted. Desired. A sexual craving to stand before a mirror and look at herself dressed only in these black lace panties. Perhaps she wanted something more. If so, she didn't confess it. She began to search the apartment—which had now become immense—to find a satisfactory mirror. She wandered long halls, passing a theater in which I sat alone, watching a movie that was some marriage between Disney's *Bambi* and his *Cinderella*. She wandered on, coming finally to a magnificent bathroom, all tiled—walls, floor, ceiling—plants decorating the corners. The color was peachy, highlighted with black. The light was gold. The mirror was on the far wall. She would have to stand up on the toilet to see herself full length. Just as she climbed up into her image— glimpsing her hair, dark, curled, cut short, her body, clad not only in the sheer lace panties but also in a tight black satin bra that made her breasts bulge—just at that moment, swept by a wave of uncharacteristic narcissistic ecstasy, she saw that Murphy was with her in the room. Stretched out on the peach-tiled shelf behind her (I saw a corpse on a slab when she said this), he eyed her. He was fully clothed, but his fly was unzipped and his desire for what he was looking at rose up naked from his pants. She stepped down again to the floor and turned to face him. He was standing, zipping up. They stood face to face, a few feet apart. He leered. Carefully, deliberately, he closed his overcoat and buttoned it. At exactly that moment trashmen in the street banged the bins so loudly that she woke. Vivid in her suddenly wakened consciousness was the eye-level closeup of Murphy's fine graceful fingers (have I mentioned Murphy's ivory-cool fingers?) slowly slipping a button through its hole. The entire sequence of the dream rose distinctly to her mind. Only for an instant was she annoyed at being wakened. If she'd slept through, she said, she'd never have known how absolutely Murphy had shut her out.

DERBY DAY

When Murphy organized a betting pool around the Kentucky Derby, Elizabeth called him a natural born bookie and bought in for a dollar. After all the lots were sold he threw the names into a hat, and Elizabeth drew Affirmed. Jack and Maude (dressed in gauze, her husband in town but not in evidence) left the party. He must have smiled at her in the afternoon shadows, then repeated the answer he got when he asked Murphy how he felt about her going: a deep sigh, a little smile, then Murphy muttered, "I forgot to remember she belongs to someone else."

Maude will have laughed. Somewhat sadly. More and more about her can be seen to have this somewhat. Somewhat sadly. Somewhat happily. Somewhat married. Somewhat free. "They all say that," she says. Then somewhat happily, "Even you would say that," smiling, "if I gave you half the chance."

Jack laughs. Happily. Happy Jack. "We're too much alike."

"How easy it was," she says.

"How easy it always is," says Jack.

After the race was won, watching Elizabeth, radiant with her victory (she read omens into anything), Murphy recalled those words said to Jack and asked himself if they were true. Most likely they were. Who can suffer, does.

He smiled then. Here they were left, he and she. Sharers in each other's secrets, less by choice than by chance. He toasted her, this thought in mind, and said goodbye.

George wandered Egypt, Maude left for Boston with her husband, and shortly after, Murphy went home to the Bronx to wait out the summer with his mother.

FUTURES

George was in town for a week early in August, not to return again until fall. He saw her over an afternoon beer. "It matters where you live," he said. It may have meant one thing, may have meant another. "No more miseries," he told her. She didn't seem quite sure what he meant. Neither was he. He dropped it. They made no allusion to what had been between them. It was or wasn't to be again. Neither asked, neither said. He showed her the marks on his neck where the night before someone had tried to strangle him in a bar.

She'd been talking of leaving. "You don't want to leave," he said. He was right. She didn't. She looked at the hairs on his chest. He told her to call his landlord. They went out into the sunshine. She had an errand to run, seemed to want to escape him, not to linger on another goodbye. "See you when you get back," she said. She squeezed his hand.

HOW WE FELT
ABOUT HER PASSING

I was off in Canada, living my summer in hermitage, still obsessed with Jack. Murphy'd retreated to the Bronx, obsessed with Maude. George and Elizabeth, too old, too wise, too worn to admit obsession, spent their separate summers quietly refining conscience, stripping away reservations, preparing for an undefined return. Just before Labor Day she put a hundred-dollar deposit on the apartment next to his, then went home to visit her mother. She sent me a postcard: "The overcoat was my father's." The Pope died that summer, and while she was out there the new Pope was invested. She cried watching the ceremony, knowing she was forever outside. (To me it made no difference, nor I imagine did it to Murphy. I didn't watch it, and neither, I'm sure, did he. The Pope's the Pope, after all, mouthpiece of the On High. What can it matter what man he was before his office or what ceremonies surround his transformation?) A few days later, Elizabeth kissed her mother goodbye and boarded the DC-10. There were no survivors. Perhaps it seems arbitrary, a cheap shot. Some resolution. No resolution at all. "So what else is new, baby?" Murphy might have said. Has anyone ever resolved a life before dying? Among her father's effects the summer before, she and her mother had found two recent, incompletely drafted letters, one to

Elizabeth, arguing the merits of career advice she'd repeatedly refused, the other to Jimmy Carter, complaining against the flawed integrity of his local Internal Revenue agents. Won't there always be something left undone? You've read to where she left us. There's no good wondering what might have happened if the plane had brought her safely back. It didn't. Even the new Pope was dead within a month. Remember Murphy's Law. Or, as Maude so often said, always laughing, never quite happily, "C'est la God damned vie."

CATHERINE GAMMON

Catherine Gammon has been publishing short fiction in diverse literary magazines since 1977.

When we asked her about the origins of this story, she wrote us: "I engage in telling reluctantly. But in fact this story has an anecdotal origin. In its first conception it was an act of preventive magic. I was about to fly west and was experiencing an extreme fear of flying. Unused to fear of flying, I was superstitious enough to take the fear as some kind of warning. Logical imagination (or imaginative logic) suggested that beginning a story in which the main character died in a plane crash—from word one—would indicate for those who survived me that I had known the plane would come down. Which, of course, would prevent it from doing so. Needless to say, the plane didn't crash, and over time I completed the story."

Gammon works as a free-lance copy editor and a part-time employee of the New York Review of Books. *Just before going to press, we learned that her first novel,* Isabel out of the Rain, *was going to be published by* Mercury House in 1991.

NORMA

NORMA

William Gilson

NORMA SAID GOOD-
BYE TO WENDELL IN THE MORNING AT A COFFEE
shop near the interstate and headed east, back to Connecticut. She had been in New York State five days, though she'd
planned to be there only one. She drove fast, something she
almost never did, and she couldn't stop doing it: no sooner
would she notice how fast the car was going and ease up on
the gas, when she'd wake to the realization that she was again
doing eighty.

Norma was not going directly home. She would have
liked to do just that—drive straight to Hartford, to her
small apartment, take a slow bath while drinking iced tea.
But she had promised to visit her parents. This meant a
detour to Millville, to the house on Greene Street where she'd
grown up.

It was a hot August day; Norma drove with the windows
open and her skirt pulled up on her thighs. She had gone to
Pelter, New York, to the funeral of Muriel Brentano, her old

college roommate, who had been hit head-on by a drunk driver.

To Norma's surprise, Wendell, Muriel's boyfriend during college, had also come. Now heavy and balding, a fire extinguisher salesman with a wife and two kids, he'd driven from his home in western Pennsylvania. After the funeral both Norma and Wendell had gone back to the Brentano house; amongst the crowd of strangers both drank more than they were used to (Wendell normally didn't drink at all), and she had gone to his motel with him and spent the night.

Norma had not slept with a man in over two years; Wendell had never been unfaithful to his wife. In the morning they made love again, and at Norma's suggestion Wendell called his wife and said that the car had broken down, major work was needed, and he couldn't get home before the end of the week. Norma called the insurance office where she was a secretary and took the rest of the week off. Then for four days they drove around the countryside, staying in motels.

Now as she made her way back, passing fields where men with machines were cutting hay and the smell of hay came in with the breeze, it seemed she was already remembering a past that was beginning to get old. As she neared the Hudson River she felt in her stomach the familiar touch of unease that was prelude to seeing her parents, and driving across the bridge her old vertigo threatened; she gripped the wheel, didn't look to either side. By the time the long curves of Route 84 took her through Danbury and then Southbury, and as the exit to Millville neared, she grew nervous, and angry with herself for being nervous.

•   •   •

In the driveway Norma let the engine idle until her father, wearing a white tee shirt, baggy khaki shorts, slippers with black socks, opened the screen door and stepped out onto the porch, smiling. Norma turned the key and in the sudden quiet got out, saying, "Hi, Dad!" Carrying her small suitcase, she met him at the top of the stairs and they hugged.

"How are you?" he said.

"A little tired, but okay."

He peered at her closely. "You look a little weak around the gills. I think drunk drivers should get life, at least."

"So do I. How're you?"

"Very well. Or, at least not so bad."

They stood in the hot sun on the porch, facing the small yard, talking. They delayed entering the living room.

"The yard looks dry," Norma said.

"It is dry. No rain. Of course, I save the water for the garden."

"Of course."

"Well, come on in, Norma. Say hello to you-know-who."

Entering behind her father, Norma paused, resisting her next breath. In the darkened living room her mother, very pale, very thin, sat in front of a large, loud color television.

"Oh, there she is," the old woman said in a reedy voice, lifting her arms, holding them for Norma to come and be hugged.

"Hello, Helen," Norma said, kissing her mother on the cheek.

"Well. So you've come to see your old mother one last time before she dies."

In the dimness Norma looked at her. It was more than two months since she'd seen her, but again there was no change. She had been dying now for almost three years, but since the first failure, when it seemed for a few weeks she'd die any day, her body held to the state Norma saw now: dark shiny eyes, translucent skin, toothless mouth, dry thinning hair. And the odor of incontinence, which Norma knew would come back to her unexpectedly and repeatedly for days after she resumed her life in Hartford.

As her father took the suitcase into Norma's room her mother looked up and said, "Well, last night was a night. Oh, my. I thought the pain would tear the heart right out of me. I called and called to your father, but do you think he'd come? Oh, no. Sound asleep as usual. So I phoned Lorne and sure enough he said, 'Helen, just hang on another minute, I'll be right there.' Bless his heart. At least someone cares. He got in his car, that dangerous Buick, and he raced over here—"

"All right, Helen," Norma's father said, coming back down the hall. "Norma won't want to hear all that again. She's come to visit us. Let's try and be nice to her, eh?" And to Norma: "Like some tea?"

"Sure."

"Water!" Helen shrieked. "Harry! Quick! Water!"

"Your water's right there. Right on your table where it belongs."

"Not that! It's gone sour! It tastes like you-know-what!"

Norma laughed. "Helen, water doesn't go sour."

"The water is fresh, Helen," her father said. "I just put it there. But I'll get more if you need it."

"I'll get it, Dad." Norma picked up the glass.

As they went into the kitchen the old woman called after them, "That's right! That's right! Just ignore me! Everybody else does!"

Returning with a glass of water, Norma said, "Helen, there is no one else around here. Dad and I are the only people in the house besides you."

"There's Lorne and Arnold."

"Oh, Helen." Norma set the glass down, pulled up a chair.

"Could I turn off the TV for a minute? We could have a visit."

"Lorne's dead," her mother said, leaning forward and twisting one of the color adjustment knobs.

Norma looked at the screen. "The picture's all purplish, Helen. It's horrible."

"In his coffin, he looked handsome. The image of health. That's what everybody says. He was my brother but I hated him. Like shit."

"Helen." Norma turned the television off.

"No!" Her mother glared at her.

"Yes," Norma said calmly.

"No," Helen said weakly.

"Now." Norma touched her mother's arm. "How are you? Are you feeling any better?"

"Shit-poo."

"Helen, are you going to be nice? Or are you going to chase me away? I've come to visit you."

"You want me to die."

"No I don't. I love you."

"Well you're the only one that does. Nobody else around here does."

"The only other person here is Dad. He loves you."

"At night, he sticks pins in me."

"Oh, really? Where does he stick the pins?"

"My ears."

"Does it hurt?"

"I scream bloody murder. Didn't you hear me last night?"

"I wasn't here last night. I've been in New York State. An old friend of mine died."

"Lorne."

"No, not Lorne. Muriel. Muriel Brentano. I went to college with her. You met her, Helen. Do you remember?"

"He never gives me any food, Norma. I haven't had a bite to eat in a week."

"Are you hungry?"

"Yes."

"Would you like me to get you something?"

"Yes."

"What?"

"Raisins."

"You'd like some raisins? Are you sure you can eat raisins?"

"Yes."

"Okay. I'll see about it. Want some tea as well?"

The old woman, reaching for the television, didn't answer. Norma stood and went into the kitchen.

"She says you've been sticking pins in her ears."

"Oh, yeah." Her father was filling two tea cups. "I'm quite the one for pins."

"She wants some raisins, Dad."

"She can't have raisins. She wouldn't eat them anyhow. And she won't drink tea. Let's go outside."

The garden was slightly smaller than in past years, but as always was weedless, the straight rows mulched with straw.

"I thought you said the drought had hurt it."

"It has. You just don't see. This garden is suffering."

He showed it to her row by row, explaining this year's changes, pointing out the dry brown edges of the pepper leaves, his arm reaching automatically to pinch off a tomato leaf, his foot nudging a bit of mulch closer to a stalk. As she followed him, half-listening, she began to feel, against her will and in spite of the old beauty of the garden, the familiar mixture of boredom and irritation she associated with visits home. Watching him as he stooped and pushed aside some wide dark-green leaves to show her a small squash, he seemed a pitiable old man. Then suddenly she felt such a rush of love for him that she almost cried, but instead spoke:

"What does the doctor say, Dad?"

"Not much he hasn't already." He stood up, grimacing as he straightened his back. "Progressing normally, what-ever the damn hell that means. I don't trust him. But then I don't trust any of them, as you know. I give him vegetables. Sometimes I think that's why he comes."

"She looks the same."

"Acts the same, too."

He turned and walked down a row, spying something in the string beans that needed looking at.

Always it had been he who was the odd one. When Norma was a child his penchant for making bizarre gadgets had seemed sometimes terrible, such as the birdfeeder with a tiny wooden grinning cat's face mounted in such a way that the face—a leering tomcat—moved side to side as the wind turned the feeder, as if the cat were watching the pecking birds. Or the sled he built her which made it appear she was sliding on it backwards down the hill. He had seemed honestly puzzled when she came home after using it only once, crying because she'd been ridiculed. Helen had under-stood, had bought her a new one.

"I'm going to pick some stuff for supper," her father

said, coming back toward her. "Just a few—"

"I'll do it, Dad."

"—carrots, maybe. We can mash 'em up for Helen. And some salad stuff."

"I'll do it."

"Okay. See you inside."

Norma knelt and pulled up a dozen carrots. She held them by the green tops and swung them one by one against the palm of her hand to shake off the dirt. She carefully brushed off one and ate it, feeling tiny bits of dirt between her teeth. Then she lay down on her back on the straw, pulling her skirt halfway up her thighs.

It was quiet, the summer afternoon quiet of the old neighborhood.

Wendell was somewhere on the highway, alone in his car. Going home.

What did she think of Wendell? He was certainly overweight. But then so was she, a little. He had changed from the days when he was Muriel's boyfriend, college days when he'd been trim and played fast-pitch softball. Then he had looked so straight—had eschewed all hippiness—and Norma had thought him headed for business success, money. None of which had happened. He was now a fire extinguisher salesman, father of two boys, married to a woman named Sally who taught kindergarten. But Wendell was better now, nicer. "Enriched by failure," she said to herself, then immediately took it back. His life was the opposite of failure. He had everything one could want: family, job, a home; and now he even had a short harmless love affair to look back on in secret.

Norma could imagine herself married to Wendell. Or someone like him. It was what she wanted. But probably would not get. Who was there to marry? In six years she'd be forty. She wasn't pretty. She didn't keep her body in shape, didn't exercise enough. Yet Wendell had liked her body. She had given old Wendell a good time. Had given herself a good time too. It was nice to know it could happen. She wondered if she would hear from him. Would he call her? She had promised not to call him even though he'd given her his office number. She'd protested, insisting she wouldn't call. And she had made him promise not to call her. This was all part of her "goodness," her self-sacrificingness. The part of herself she most hated.

If she were so good, so self-sacrificing, why didn't she move back to Millville and help her father take care of her mother?

And if she were so good, what should she make of her treatment of Muriel, her old friend? After the first shock, after the funeral, she had hardly thought of Muriel at all.

"Norma!"

Her father's voice from the back stairs startled her. She sat up, her heart beating.

"I need the carrots!"

"Sure, Dad!" She stood, brushing bits of straw off her skirt.

As soon as Norma and her father sat at the kitchen table Helen turned the television up full.

"God!" Norma put her hands over her ears. "Dad, that's horrible."

She went into the living room, turned it down. Helen glared fiercely up at her.

Norma glared back. "No," she said as if to a child. "Helen, you cannot do that."

"Shit-poo." Helen spat the words but left the volume down.

"Sorry, Norma," her father said as she sat down. "It's a new tactic she's on to. I usually just let 'er do it. It's as hard on her as it is on me."

"Can't you just make her turn it down?"

"If it was me who did what you just did, she would've started screaming. I'd rather have the damn neighbors hear the TV than hear her scream. She cranks it down eventually."

Again the volume went up.

Again Norma went in, turned it down.

Coming back into the kitchen, she laughed.

"Dad, it's crazy."

"You said it. Sometimes I think I'm crazier than her."

"I don't think you are."

"But it's possible."

They ate in silence for perhaps five minutes when Helen yelled, "Harry! I'm soaking wet!"

Her father sighed. He closed his eyes, rubbing his temples. Raising his voice, he said, "Helen, I'll be right there." And to Norma: "She does it on purpose. God damn it to hell. She hasn't really lost control. She does it to be mean."

"Harry!" the old woman yelled, "it's running off the rubber!"

"I'll help you, Dad."

Together they eased Helen onto the wheelchair, wheeled her into the bathroom. He had had the old small bathroom with its floor of little hexagonal white tiles done over to make it easier to care for his wife; now it reminded Norma of the ladies room where she worked.

While her father took the rubber pad into the backyard and hosed it down, and took the blanket downstairs to the washer, Norma removed her mother's robe and nightgown, unsnapped the big absurd-looking diaper. Then she wheeled her mother into the bedroom and lifted her onto the hospital bed.

Norma breathed through her mouth as she worked. She tried to close off her sense of touch, even at moments let her eyes go slightly out of focus. The old woman stared angrily at the ceiling, silently cooperative. Norma cleaned and powdered her, put on a fresh diaper and a nightgown. When she had finished she kissed the old woman's forehead.

"All set, Helen."

"You wish I was dead."

"No. I love you."

The old woman's voice was hoarse: "You're the only one that does."

"Helen, stop it. We love you. Dad loves you."

"Shit-poo."

"You sound tired. Why don't you stay here for the night? It's getting to be your bedtime. Take your pill and call it a day, huh?"

"Not on your life. Suppose there's a storm?"

"A storm?"

"Snow's predicted."

"Well, so what? You're safe in here."

"Norma, when are you getting married?"

"I'm not."

"They told me you're getting married."

"They're wrong."

"You'll wait till I'm stone dead, that's when. I'll be fresh in my grave and away you'll go."

"Stop it, Helen."

"I think there's a man in your room."

"Oh? Really?"

"Is he the one?"

"What one?"

"The one to marry. What're you waiting for?"

"Helen, stop it. I don't want to talk about this. I'm tired."

"Lorne said to me just this morning, 'Helen,' he said, 'Norma's got a man she keeps in her room. They're waiting.' And I said, 'I know it, Lorne. Oh for the love of God don't I know it. How that girl hates her mother.' "

"Helen, I am not going to listen to this craziness. Lorne is dead. There is no man in my room."

"I hear him in there. I hear his shoes creaking. You want me to go to sleep so you can go in there—"

"Helen, listen. Shut up. Do you hear me? Shut up."

"He stands in the closet in the dark."

"Shut up! Shut the hell up!"

"You want me to die."

"I want you to shut up! I want you to stop it! Leave me alone! And leave Dad alone! You evil bitch!"

She turned and left, slammed the door.

From behind the closed door the old woman yelled, "Harry! Har-ry!"

Norma, crying, met her father in the kitchen; he was carrying the rubber pad and a sponge.

"Norma, what's the matter?"

"Her!"

"What?"

"She's so god-damned crazy. She's evil. Honestly, sometimes I really do hate her. I slammed the door. I'm going outside."

She continued on through the kitchen, not waiting for

his answer. Outside it was getting dark and she sat in a lawnchair.

It was quiet. Lights in the neighborhood houses were beginning to come on. Her crying subsided, she found a tissue in the pocket of her skirt, blew her nose.

She felt tired. Her body suddenly ached. Leaning her head against the back of the chair, she closed her eyes.

Her father came down the stairs, waking her from the beginnings of sleep.

"I'm tired," she said to him. "I've got to go to bed."

He sat down. "Sorry about that, Norma."

"It's not your fault. I'm not even sure it's hers. Dad, maybe it's time to think again about a home."

"Not yet." He paused. "It's not as if I don't think about it. I think about it every day. But I can handle her a while yet."

"Okay." Norma got up, kissed his cheek. "Night, Dad."

"See you in the morning."

Norma woke from a dream in which she and Wendell were treading water in a lake; they were close but not touching, facing with their mouths just above the water, talking quietly across the calm surface.

This was the room she used to wake in every morning. The very same white curtains patterned with little blue flowers. The small maple desk. The corner shelf her father had built for her record player. The full-length mirror on the back of the door.

Norma heard the television and got up.

Showering, she decided to leave soon. The weariness she felt last night had not lifted, she was due to get her period in three days, and she wanted to be alone. She dressed, packed her suitcase. In the living room Helen was staring at a Roadrunner cartoon and did not respond to Norma's "Good morning." She fixed herself orange juice and toast and coffee and carried it on a tray down the back steps. Already the morning was hot, and her father, in a sleeveless undershirt, shorts, dark socks and slippers, was watering the garden. His legs were thin and varicosed, white against a rich growth of polebeans.

"You look sexy, Dad."

"That's what they tell me." He smiled, obviously pleased to see her. In a minute he came over and sat next to her, wiping his face with a red handkerchief.

"I told her—about last night—I told her to cut that damn crap out."

"Thanks, Dad. I doubt it'll make much difference."

"Me too."

Norma sipped her coffee. "Dad, do you remember that sled you made me once? The backwards one?"

"The backwards one? Sure. The one you didn't care much for. That was years ago. You remember that?"

"Of course. How could I forget. Do you still have it?"

"What for?"

"Oh, nothing. There's someone I'd like to give it to. Someone who has kids, who'd get a kick out of it."

He laughed.

"Norma, you're too late. About ten years at least, I'd say. Maybe fifteen. I tossed that out, cleaning the cellar. I was surprised I'd even kept it that long. I'm sorry, it's a goner."

"It was just a thought."

"You leaving this morning?"

"Yes. I want to get back."

"I know, I know."

He got up, moved the water hose, came back.

"I could make you another one," he said.

"What?"

"A sled, a backwards sled. I could make you another one. Easy."

"Could you? Really?"

"Oh sure. It's mainly a matter of paint. It's an optical illusion."

"Dad—that'd be great."

Her mother said, "You come back soon, Norma. Your father needs you. He can barely take care of himself as it is. Especially with me about to die."

Through the open front door Norma could see her father putting a box of vegetables into her car.

"Helen," Norma said, "you've got some life in you yet. You'll outlive me."

"I can take the punishment."

Norma hugged her mother's thin shoulders, kissed her.

"Bye, Helen. I love you."

Outside, her father held the car door open for her; as she started the engine he said, "I put an eggplant in there. Nice fat one."

"Thanks, Dad."

"Call me when you get to Hartford, let me know you made it."

"Of course. Now, don't forget the sled."

"No, no."

Driving up Route 84, approaching Hartford, Norma laughed to herself. She would send Wendell the sled. Sometime toward the end of the year, as Christmas approached, a large package would arrive at his office. Inside he'd find the backward sled. She would enclose a short letter, explaining what it was.

She pictured him holding the sled, remembering her.

And then what would Wendell do? Call her? Get in his car and come see her? You could never tell.

W I L L I A M   G I L S O N

We heard about Bill Gilson through the Fine Arts Work Center in Provincetown, Massachusetts. He sent us the story "Norma," which we liked immediately. Regarding the making of it, he said, " 'Norma' began with an image, an image of a woman driving over a bridge—it was that very long high bridge where Interstate 84 crosses the Hudson River. She was coming back from a funeral, and she felt compelled by duty to stop and visit her parents in Connecticut. Also, I remember early on picturing Norma's father standing on the front porch in his shorts. Norma's mother came out of nowhere, right from the start threatening to take over the story."

Gilson has these visions in Cambridge, Mass., where he lives, writes, and works (at MIT). A collection of his poems, There She Goes, *was published a few years ago, and his story "Getting Through It Together" was included in* The Pushcart Prize VII. *Every month he writes a column for* New England Farmer *magazine.*

MUCHO ABOUT THE NADA

MUCHO ABOUT THE NADA

Lori Anne Hackel

STELLA GODFREY IS SITTING IN THE ONCOLOGIST'S WAITING ROOM WITH her girlfriend Miranda Long. When the nurse calls Miranda's name, Stella thinks she can provide some moral support and goes in with her.

The walk down the hallway is not reassuring. There are no doors on the examining rooms, just an additional section of white wall jutting halfway across the open space between one room and the next. The plaster walls and high ceilings are all painted white. At the end of the hall there are floor-to-ceiling windows, and two ficus trees stand positioned like sentries at either end. Stella guesses they are trying for an overall effect of calm, cool, openness, but everyone knows that white means death. And the openness, the lack of doors sends a shiver down her spine at what she suspects is an indifferent cruelty to people who need privacy the most: those suffering, in pain and dying.

Miranda sits in a schoolroom chair, the kind with an arm extended to form a square, paddlelike top for writing.

The doctor comes in, and as soon as Stella sees him she decides she must convince Miranda to get a second opinion. He is wearing a powder-blue, checked shirt, a wide, black belt, and brown plaid pants. A shock of red hair stands high on his receding forehead and bushes out around two prominent ears. Stella thinks if he can't even figure out what shirt goes with what pants how will he ever know what treatment is the right one for Miranda's disease?

"Hello, Miranda," he says, looking at her chart. "How have you been since I last saw you? Any dizziness, nausea, difficulty in breathing, loss of appetite?" His pen trembles over her chart.

Miranda says, "All of the above," and flashes him a dazzling smile. For a smoker, she has the most beautiful white teeth.

Unfortunately, the good doctor is too busy scribbling to appreciate them. Stella can see two little drops of white foam forming at the corners of his mouth.

The nurse comes in and takes Miranda out to be weighed.

"Excuse me, Doctor," Stella says.

He looks up from Miranda's chart. His red eyebrows are zig-zagged out like two lightning bolts. "Are you a relation?" he asks. He seems surprised that she should be addressing him.

"No." She hesitates. "I'm not. But I wanted to ask you something concerning my friend, Miranda."

"I've been in contact with a Mr. . . ." He looks back down at the chart, puts his finger on it, and says, "O'Leary, Mrs. Long's father, I believe." He glances up at her as if for confirmation. "If you have any questions, please direct them to him. He knows everything about Mrs. Long's condition." He closes the folder, says, "Excuse me," and hastens out of the room.

The nurse brings Miranda back in. Her arm is linked through Miranda's, and Stella can't tell whether it's to give Miranda support or to keep her from trying to escape. "Lost two more pounds," Miranda says, and sinks slowly into the chair.

The nurse inserts a needle into Miranda's hand. Stella imagines a drug looking much like little Pac Mans chasing the bad cells in a race against time through the maze of blood vessels in Miranda's body. All of a sudden she feels the terror and pity of it all and bolts out of the room. She rushes into the ladies' room, slams the stall door, sits on the toilet and puts her head between her knees.

Miranda is waiting for her when she comes out. "Are you all right?"

"Sure," Stella says. "I think I must have eaten too many prunes this morning. A new diet I've been trying. You're not allowed to eat anything but fruit until lunch time."

Miranda takes her arm. "Before you take me home, I want to go to Sleeping Meadows."

"Listen, Miranda. There's something I've got to tell you. What did that doctor say to you? It doesn't matter. What matters is that you get a second opinion. I don't trust him. Everyone gets a second opinion these days. It's like buying a house or a new car. You never go with the first one."

Miranda looks at her. "Will you take me to Sleeping Meadows?"

It was four years ago when Stella first met Miranda. She had been looking for a new hairdresser. Hers had quit to pursue what he thought would be the new, hot trend in nail care: drive-through nail salons complete with play areas. They were targeted towards those suburban housewives who couldn't afford babysitters but still cared about having great-looking nails.

The opening of Miranda's beauty salon was the culmination of a lifelong dream. It came after twenty-five years of working in makeup. She had sold door-to-door for Avon, worked behind the cosmetics counter at Robinson's, and had her own makeup area in several beauty salons around the city.

Stella had never seen a beauty salon like Miranda's. It was furnished all in antiques, from the armoire at the entrance for coats to the cabinets each operator had in which to store their scissors, blow-dryers, hair spray, rollers, papers, and pins. There were country-print papers on the walls and matching prints on the sofas and chairs. The floors were wood peg and groove, the coffeepot was sterling silver, and the cups and saucers were bone china. Baskets of green ficus trees and dripping grape ivy plants were everywhere.

Miranda greeted her at the door and offered a free, complimentary lip wax. And as soon as the pain stopped and she could feel her lip again they began to talk. They discovered that they were both the same age, forty-three, and had been born and raised in L.A. They were both from poor families, and whenever Stella came into the salon after that they would exchange poor childhood stories. Sometimes, on Mondays, when the salon was closed, they'd go out to lunch together.

When Miranda got sick, the salon, as if it were a living part of Miranda, also started to deteriorate. Miranda, ill from chemotherapy, cancelled appointments or simply failed to show up. Some of the beauty operators quit, and new ones weren't hired. Customers stopped coming.

Eventually, Miranda was forced to sell out. To cheer her up, Stella would often say, "When you get well, we'll open our own place. You'll do makeup, and I'll sell books."

Selling books was all she could think of to do. Except for raising two children, both now away at college, and performing other housewifely duties, the only other thing she ever did was sit in bed and read. When the children were young, she'd read at night, but at the time she met Miranda she was definitely in the bed more than she was out of it. She didn't see anything peculiar in that. A lot of her girlfriends were spending more time in bed. It made no difference that her girlfriends' bed time was with men, usually not their husbands, and hers was with a book. It was all somehow tied up with that mid-life crisis syndrome. What was important was the desire for bed.

Stella figured if she couldn't have Woody Allen, the only man she knew of who could make her laugh about dying, then the next best thing was a book by a male author who made her laugh.

"This Golden Freeway has really kept up with the times, hasn't it?" Stella says to Miranda. "It kind of reminds me of the Constitution in that respect. Years ago the word 'golden' referred to the sunshine. And the word still applies today, to that wonderful yellow haze we've come to be blessed with. Smog. It sound almost lyrical, doesn't it? I love that word. 'Smog.'" She repeats it several more times.

Miranda says, "On a clear day the view from the top of Sleeping Meadows is really breathtaking. My plot is up there. I want to show it to you. Have you and Ernest picked yours out yet?"

Oh I've picked my plot out, Stella thinks, and it's not six feet underground, either. It includes at least forty-five more years of living, which brings her up to age ninety, some grandchildren, and maybe even a face-lift along the way.

"If you haven't," Miranda is saying, "I recommend you do. It's really not too soon. All the good ones are going fast."

What is this, Stella wonders, an after-Christmas sale where all the best buys are bought up in the first five minutes of the store opening? The last time she heard of a good buy it was on fake fur car seat covers. She didn't care about getting the good buy then and she certainly doesn't want to feel she should get one now. "Good buy" reminds her of good-by. She looks over at her friend and wonders what she's thinking. She's always so calm and composed. Stella has never heard her utter one complaint in the two years since her cancer was diagnosed.

On the day before her mastectomy she actually had a party in her hospital room. Stella had wracked her brains over what gift to bring her. Candy was out. Miranda never ate sweets. She had once told Stella that sugar had made her sick as a child. Personally, Stella thinks Miranda is anorexic in her head, and has psyched herself out against sweets. She was thin, even before getting sick. A nightgown? Miranda was very picky about her clothes, and Stella was afraid of choosing the wrong thing. A book? That's what Stella would have liked, but she had never seen Miranda read anything heavier than *Vogue*. Of course, it was true that its September issue is almost as weighty as *War and Peace*.

She finally decided on flowers. Miranda loved fresh-cut flowers. What better gift? Not from a florist, either. Home-grown. It was as close to a part of herself as she could get. There was only one problem. Stella's yard didn't have any.

She'd never had any flowers, even though she told the gardener many times how much she loved them. She can't figure it out. Maybe he doesn't like them, which seems ridiculous. How can a gardener not like flowers? What's more likely is that he can't understand her. There is definitely a slight language barrier between them. Here's how their conversation went the time Miranda was due to go into the hospital.

Stella was in the kitchen cleaning up the lunch dishes when she heard the roar of that infernal blower. It was followed by José coming around the bend and into the backyard. He had the blower tucked under his arm and was taking aim at the few scattered dead leaves as if he were Rambo with his M-60 (a movie she would have never seen except it was Ernest's turn to choose). Stella wondered if it were Hemingway who introduced the word "macho" into the everyday American male vocabulary. "Nada" was another word Hemingway loved. To him, a person died with dignity if he was macho when he faced the great nada. Stella couldn't decide whether Hemingway was macho or cowardly by committing suicide. She was afraid she would whine in protest and self-pity when it came her turn to face the great nada.

She tapped on the window to get José's attention, but of course it was useless. He walked around the patio, blowing a few more leaves to smithereens, then disappeared around the other side of the house. Stella dried her hands and rushed out the front door to intercept him before he could escape.

"José!" She yelled, even though she was standing directly behind him.

He turned around and switched off the blower.

"Hi," she said.

He pulled the red-and-white neckerchief from his nose and mouth, and lifting his straw hat said, "Hi." His face was brown and creased around the eyes.

So far, so good, she thought. We understood each other perfectly.

"Can you plant me some flowers?"

"I don't understand." He enunciated each word slowly, then laughed, revealing a silver front tooth.

She pointed to the pink and white rosebushes in her next-door neighbor's yard. "Flowers," she said, trying to think of the word in Spanish. Suddenly the word "flores" burst from her.

"Yes," he said, and smiled.

"For *moi*," she said, slapping her chest.

"You like it?"

"Yes." She nodded her head up and down like a yo-yo.

"Okay," he said, and turned the blower back on.

She still hasn't seen any flowers.

On the night before she was to visit Miranda in the hospital, she put a flashlight on the table by her bed and set the clock radio very low for five A.M. When Ernest asked what the flashlight was for, she said if there was an earthquake in the middle of the night, the power was sure to go out, and she wouldn't be able to find her way to the bathroom.

She was up before the alarm, switched it off, and felt for her robe at the end of the bed. She tied the belt extra tight and grabbing the flashlight, slipped off the bed. The scissors and tennis shoes were right where she put them, under the bed, next to the dust ruffle. She tiptoed to the front door, jammed her feet into the tennis shoes, lifted the dead-bolt, and let herself out.

It was very cold at that predawn hour, and she was tempted to go back to get a jacket, but if Ernest awoke, she wasn't sure if he'd believe her story about going out to catch the paper boy to tell him to stop throwing the paper on the wet lawn. Even though Ernest likes macho movies, he is honest. He would never approve of her picking (stealing, he'd call it) her neighbor's flowers, even if they were for a friend who was dying.

She crept under her neighbor's living room window and switched off the flashlight. Her feet sank into the soft, wet lawn. She put the flashlight into her pocket and took out the scissors. Her hands were sweating, and the grass blades pricked at her ankles like so many cold needles as she cut the pink and white roses.

Shivering and sweating, she stumbled with the prickly roses back into her own yard. At the front yard she pulled off the muddy tennis shoes and carried them with the flowers into the laundry area. She dropped the tennis shoes on the floor and put the flowers in a vase of water. She set the vase on top of the washer and closed the sliding door. It was five-twenty when she got back into bed. Ernest never moved.

Five hours later she was walking down the hospital hallway towards Miranda's room. The vase was clutched to her chest while perspiration dripped down her arms, bleaching her sweater from red to pink. How was she going to be up, bright, and optimistic? At the doorway to Miranda's room she froze.

Miranda was sitting up in bed. She had on a pink-and-white bed jacket with lace around the collar and cuffs of the sleeves. Her face shone with pink blush and lip gloss, and her black hair flowed about her shoulders. She held a paper cup of champagne in her hand. A very handsome male nurse had pulled up a chair so that it was positioned right next to her shoulder. "Ah, Miranda," he said. "If only I wasn't gay. I'd marry you in a minute."

She always had that effect on men.

Miranda and Donna, a heavyset woman with short blonde hair and black roots, laughed. Donna was one of the beauty operators from Miranda's shop. Miranda's ex-husband was also there. He was slouched against the back corner with his hands shoved deep into his pockets. He did not laugh and neither did the gray-headed woman sitting in the chair at the foot of the bed. Stella had never seen this woman before and guessed her to be Donna's mother. She was wearing a blue polyester pants suit and had a pair of half-glasses hanging from a cord around her neck. They were the kind that bookkeepers, and other people who do close work, buy in drugstores. But the way they rested on the woman's chest reminded Stella of a baby in one of those infant carriers that young mothers wear. They seemed such an intimate part of her.

When Miranda saw Stella standing in the doorway she said, "Where in the world did you get those gorgeous flowers? I don't think I ever saw any so large."

"Only for you," Stella said. She came into the room and set them on the table next to the bed.

"We were just having a little before-the-surgery party. Roberto, would you pour a drink for my friend Stella?"

Stella looked around the room. "Are you sure it's all right to drink?"

"I think we're all over twenty-one here. I won't say how much over."

"I mean for you," Stella said. "Is it all right for you, before surgery?"

"Why not? Maybe I'll even drink enough to where I

won't need any anesthesia. Wouldn't that be great?" She laughed and took a sip of champagne.

"Miranda, my psychic would like to look at your palm," Donna said.

"Okay, but it'll have to be the right one." She set the paper cup on the table. "My left, as you can see, is already engaged." She looked up at the I.V. bottle. "I hope the right's the one with the long life line."

Stella had a sudden morbid thought: everyone to the right goes to the gas chamber and everyone to the left gets to work to death in the camp. What's the difference?

The gray-haired woman rose from her chair and, tugging her jacket down, moved to the head of the bed. She put her glasses on and took Miranda's outstretched palm. Stella was thinking that if she were going to have surgery, she'd be so worried about not waking up from the anesthesia and what else they might find that she'd have to take a Valium to calm down. Maybe they didn't allow Valium, and that's why Miranda was drinking champagne.

The psychic lifted her head from Miranda's palm and frowned.

Miranda looked her in the face and said, "This woman looks like she could use a drink. Would someone please pour one for her?"

The psychic shook her head and stepped backwards towards the door.

After Donna took her away, Stella said, "I don't believe in those people. I know how they operate. I have a friend who once hired one for a party. And she told him to be sure to tell the guests only pleasant things. She wanted everyone to have a good time."

Stella took Valium when she got home from the hospital. She awoke later with a headache.

Miranda awoke from her surgery minus her left breast, and got more bad news.

That was two years ago.

Now they are standing on the top of the hill at Sleeping Meadows Cemetery. Miranda says, "I wanted you to see this. I only hope the day will be sunny like today." She looks out towards the mountains.

Stella follows her gaze. The dark, rounded convolutions look like the backs of women's heads. Their thick hair tumbles down to the city below. This image, of a row of women standing side by side, united and protecting, somehow gives her comfort.

"The coffin is white and gold with pink satin lining. It'll be surrounded with bouquets of pink and white flowers." She points to the spot where Stella imagines the head of the coffin will be. "I want you to sit there," she says. "So you can see me." She looks at Stella. "When you take me home, I'll show you my dress."

"No," Stella says, turning her back. "I mean, surprise me."

"There's no need to be superstitious," Miranda says. "It's not like a wedding dress where there'd be bad luck. Is it the bride who shows the dress or the person who sees it before the wedding who gets the bad luck? I know if someone sees a bride on her wedding day that person will have good luck, but I can't remember the other, can you?"

"No," Stella says, as the grotesque image of Miss Havisham in her decayed wedding dress dances before her eyes. This conversation is depressing, this lumping together of weddings and funerals all in the same breath. Lump. She does not like that word. Furtively her hands feel her breasts, pinching between thumb and forefinger lumps of flesh.

Miranda takes her arm. "Come inside with me for a minute. I have something I want to give to the embalmer."

Mr. D. K. Nunn could be a Truman Capote look-alike. He is short and bald, has a bland, round face, and wears wire-rimmed glasses. He extends a pale, fleshy, well-manicured hand. "How may I be of service?" he asks, looking from Stella to Miranda. His voice is hushed and every word with an S-sound ends in a long snakelike hiss.

Miranda says. "I'm here because I want you to see what I look like now. So when the time comes you won't have to guess about it. And just in case you should forget between now and then, I've brought you this."

She reaches in her handbag and takes out an eight-by-ten glossy colored photo of herself. It must have been taken before she got sick because she is not wearing her wig, and her own hair looks very full.

She's worked in beauty parlors too long, Stella thinks. She's become just like those women who come in with their pictures of Joan Collins and Linda Evans torn from *People* magazine. They hand them to their hairdressers, saying, "Make me look like her."

When Miranda started to speak, the embalmer's eyes opened larger and seemed to grow enormous behind the bifocal lenses. It was as if he was seeing his chance of a lifetime. Here, finally, was a beautiful soon-to-be corpse instead of the usual aged one with gray hair, flabby skin, and rotting teeth. He puts his hand to his throat. "My dear," he says, "what many people don't realize is that when a beloved passes from this world on to the next there is something, let us call it the soul, that really does leave the body. Everyone blames us embalmers. They say their beloveds did not look that way in life. But really it is not our fault. By the time the body gets to us, it really is altered."

"But Mr. Nunn," Miranda says, "how many of these people had you met or seen before they passed on?"

He looks to Stella as if trying to confirm that he's heard correctly. "Well," he clears his throat, "none, actually."

"You see my point. Why I came here?"

"Very brave of you." He bows his head, showing a shining top sprinkled with tiny drops of perspiration.

"I've chosen a white-and-gold coffin with pink lining, and my dress is pink."

"Very beautiful." He takes a large, white handkerchief from his pants pocket and mops the top of his head.

"So of course I'd like pink lipstick and blush."

"As you wish."

"Do you need to write that down or will you remember?"

"Mrs. Long," he says, "I will never forget you." He takes her bony hand in his fleshy palm and covers it with his other hand, as if trying to protect it.

The living room of Miranda's father's apartment is cluttered with ceramic dolls. Each doll has a different face and costume, and every one of them is beautiful.

"Miranda? Is that you, honey?"

"Yes, Dad. Stella's with me." Miranda sits down on the couch. Her face is as gray as a wolf's hide.

Miranda's father comes out of the kitchen. He has a red face, blue eyes, and sparse white hair. "How'd it go?" he asks, and rushes to adjust a pillow for Miranda's head as she lies down. "You got another one of those treatments, didn't you?" He straightens up and looks down at her. "Yeah, I can see it in your eyes. Did you remember to ask that doctor how soon you can come off of that stuff?"

"He didn't say," Miranda says, closing the incriminating eyes.

He turns to Stella. "As soon as the doctor says it's okay, I'm going to take her on a trip to Hawaii. I think it'll do her a world of good, don't you? To be near the water and get a little sun. She could use some color. It's those treatments that are doing it to her."

"It's so hot in here," Miranda says. "I'm dying of thirst." She starts to laugh and chokes.

Stella goes into the kitchen. That's one thing I can prevent, she thinks. She stops at the table. It is covered with newspapers. On top of them are jars of paint, brushes, rags, and a doll. Its face is painted to look like a Japanese geisha: white skin, thin black eyebrows and thick lashes, deep brown eyes, and a red mouth. The material of her blue kimono is cotton, but has been painted to look like silk. Miranda's father took up this hobby of painting beautiful faces and exquisite clothes on ceramic dolls five years ago, after his retirement from the meat-packing industry.

Stella opens the cupboard, takes out a glass, and fills it with water for Miranda.

She carries it into the living room and sets it on the table next to Miranda's head.

Miranda says, "Dad, would you put the 'Ave Maria' record on? I want Stella to hear it."

"Sure, honey," he says, but doesn't move. He stares down at her face, as if sneaking a good look while her eyes are closed. His arms hang limp at his sides.

After a moment he turns to the record player. He takes the record out of its jacket, and holding the edges against the palms of his hands, like some sacred object, gently lays it on the turntable. He lowers the arm of the needle until it barely touches the surface of the record.

"You ladies will have to excuse me," he says, "but I've got work to do in the kitchen." At the entrance to the kitchen he glances over his shoulder at Miranda and shakes his head.

Miranda's eyes are still closed. "While you were in the bathroom," she says, "the doctor came back in. He said he'd calculated that I have about two months left. I'm going to have this played at my Mass. Isn't it beautiful?"

A mass of black hooded figures, each holding a single flower, file before Stella's eyes. It's Disney's *Fantasia*, a movie she had taken her children to see when they were young. But it's the only time she's ever heard this music. Sentimental. Disney is definitely sentimental. Then why does she feel so weak? She knows if she sits down she'll never be able to get up again. Why is this music pulling her insides out? A swift, cold pain shoots through her abdomen. The word "no" is shrieking over and over again in her head.

"I know you said no," Miranda is saying.

"What?" Had she actually been shrieking out loud?

"I know you said you didn't want to see my dress. But I would really like to show it to you. And I know you won't deny the request of a dying woman."

You've got me there, Stella thinks. There's no way to mention their book and cosmetic shop now. She'd only be fooling herself, and she wonders if that's what she's been doing all along anyway. Has Miranda been playing that game for her benefit?

"Pink, right?" Stella says.

"In a plastic bag in the back of my closet. Bring it out here."

Stella goes down the hall to Miranda's bedroom. Like Miranda, the bedroom is immaculate. There is a pink comforter on the bed. The pillow is in a starched, white case, etched with pink embroidery, and is propped against a brass headboard. The night table is round, with a glass top and a full pink skirt. On top of the night table there is a tray of cosmetics, a mirror, a lamp, and a T.V. remote control.

Stella opens the closet door. The left side of the closet has been partitioned into two sections. On the bottom rack are the slacks, each folded neatly over its own hanger. Above them are the blouses and shirts, every one completely buttoned. The dresses are on the right side of the closet. A clear, plastic bag covers each one. As Stella looks through Miranda's dresses, she has a sudden feeling of déjà vu, of searching through her mother's closet. This was twelve years ago, and Stella was looking for a dress to bury her mother in. Now she thinks how much easier it would have been had her mother left instructions. But then, her mother hadn't planned on dying. Like Miranda, her mother had cancer, but she never gave up hope, and then it was too late to make any decisions.

Miranda has accepted her fate. Stella's mother did not. But she was another one who never complained. Maybe that's the key, Stella thinks.

She finds the dress and takes it out to Miranda. "It's beautiful," she says, admiring the soft, pink folds of chiffon.

Miranda smiles. "I knew you would like it."

Two months later Stella attends Miranda's funeral. It is a sunny day, and Stella thanks nature for finally coming through for Miranda. She enters the chapel and sees the white-and-gold coffin. The lid is raised, but all Stella can see from where she is standing is the pink satin lining. People are milling in front of it, talking in subdued, hushed voices. Stella takes a seat in the middle of the last row.

The eulogy is short, and Stella thinks Miranda was not

praised as she should have been. A man gets up, probably Miranda's brother from Chicago, and announces that only family members will be going to the grave site. He thanks everyone else for coming and then calls the names of the pallbearers who will help carry the coffin.

Stella pushes her way into the aisle and begins walking rapidly up to the front. She's not even sure if the service is over. All she knows is that the coffin is going to be closed and she's got to get there before this happens. She must see and admire her friend one last time.

L O R I   A N N E   H A C K E L

Lori Anne Hackel's short story, "Mucho About the Nada," is about an issue our human nature does not confront well: death. The story is a contrast between two women, one who uses her imminent death as the ultimate black-tie affair, and her friend, who is so afraid of the prospect that she cannot face even the idea of it. The author's use of a woman's point of view highlights with satirical irony Hemingway's "macho" concept of courage.

Lori Anne Hackel lives in Encino, California, and is just starting her writing career.

OUR CHILDREN,
OUR PEERS

OUR CHILDREN, OUR PEERS

Vernon E. Jordan, Jr.

MOST COMMENCE-
MENT ADDRESSES REMIND ME OF THE FRENCH PHI-
losopher who said that "People propose to us patterns of life
which neither the proposer nor his hearers have any hope of
following, or, what is more, any desire to follow."

So I won't exhort today. Nor will I do what I have been
doing for many weeks now—making speeches suggesting
that the Surgeon General issue a warning that the Administration's budget is dangerous to the health of poor people
and minority people.

Instead, I want to talk on a more personal level. I want
to talk about the joys and the heartaches, the pleasures and
the fears, of raising children and seeing them one day as full-
grown adults, graduates of a great university.

For that is the position in which I find myself today:
that is the reason this day, so special for you, is also so
special for me. Among the graduates today is my daughter,

Vickee. That is what makes today so special, so different.

When a man's only child graduates from college, his mind runs along the course of time until it arrives at the beginnings: the joyful news that a child is on the way, the long months of anxious waiting, the shared experience of expectant parents.

I think back to the rush to the hospital, the pacing of the corridors, and finally the wonderful news that unto us a child is born, a baby girl, a fresh breeze of future gladness and promise.

I vividly remember looking through the window at my newborn baby in those early morning hours so long ago. And I remember my feeling of joyous excitement, waving frantically at that tiny bundle whose eyes were closed tightly, whose little body was exhausted with the effort of coming into this world.

Your parents will recall their similar experience when you were born. And they may also have felt what I felt at that time, amid the joy and excitement a faint feeling of disquiet; a twinge of anxiety about the question marks in life that await our children.

At the root of that feeling lay the limitless potentials symbolized by the awesome experience of birth. The writer James Agee put it so well:

> In every child who is born, under no matter what circumstances, and of no matter what parents, the potentiality of the human race is born again; and in him, too, once more, and of each of us, our terrific responsibility towards human life; towards the utmost idea of goodness, of the horror of error, and of God.

That feeling never leaves parents. Before us always are the question marks of the future; the uncertainties of life that can creep up unawares and lift our dreams high or turn them into nightmares. Yes, that anxiety is always present; always making us try harder for our children's sakes, always making us aware of their needs and guarding their futures.

Our children grow. We count each new development as landmarks in our personal histories: the day our baby takes the first step, speaks her first word, goes off to school for the first time.

We watched our children grow, and we grew with them. We stayed up nights when they were sick, and we tended their cuts and bruises. We had good days; we had bad days. We made mistakes, and hurt them in ways grown-ups can never comprehend. But we also made them happy, joining in their gay laughter on a summer's afternoon.

And as they grew older, we shared their new experiences. We tried to remember the little math we learned and the history we forgot because they needed our help with their homework. We laid down the law, and then compromised. We fought over staying out late, or the boys that turned up on our doorstep, or the clutter in the room.

Sometimes our children were rebellious and wrong. Sometimes we parents were dogmatic and wrong. Sometimes we gave our children the comfort they needed, and then, as time passed, they gave us comfort in our bad moments. Sometimes that is when the turning point comes, when the dependency shifts. For so many years I lent my daughter what strength I had, and last summer, in my time of trial and pain, it was she who brought strength to me; she who brought me the power of love and will to help me pull through.

Finally, the day comes when our children are no longer children. That is why Commencement Day is so important. It is a rite of passage, a formal declaration of independence, a passing over into the larger world.

"Commencement" seems a strange term to use for a ceremony that *ends* the years of college. But it is very apt. For "commencement" means a beginning, and this day signifies not so much the end of one's college career but the beginning of one's adult life.

This day marks the cutting of the strings, the leaving of a protected environment for the larger world. It marks a fundamental change in our relations with our children. For they are now our peers.

They have their own lives to lead, their own dreams to follow, their own aspirations to seek.

Before, we parents were center stage. Now we are in the wings, pushed back by the inevitable passage of time and circumstance, pushed back as we ourselves once pushed back our own parents, and they theirs.

So we parents, who have spent the past two decades learning and adjusting to new situations and new phases of development, must now adjust to yet another phase, perhaps the most difficult of all to accept. But our acceptance of this new order is a mark of our own maturity, and a final service to the children we love so dearly—the gift of allowing them to be themselves.

Thus far I have been talking to your parents, to my fellow fathers and mothers of this graduating class. But this is your day, and I do want to say a few things to you directly.

The first is to apologize for the world into which you graduate. It is in many ways a mean world. The superpowers rattle rockets at each other. Television brings us, between commercials for expensive cars and clothing, pictures of some of the earth's starving millions. People still judge other people by the color of their skin. Pockets of hate pollute our human environment. Right here, in the shadow of this great University, well over one out of five black people are out of work.

Yes, it is in many ways a mean, mean world. But it is not much different from the world we entered. And in some ways it is a better world. When I returned home after my college graduation, it was to separate drinking fountains, the back of the bus, and the denial of basic constitutional rights.

So the world has changed. Not nearly enough, but it has changed. And it changed because in the midst of this meanness, buried deep within the caves of injustice, there was the throbbing of the human spirit, the determination by millions of individuals that wrong is something to overcome, not to tolerate.

And so many wrongs were overcome. The many that remain are ours—together—to overcome. But the prime responsibility must be yours, for you enter this brave new world unscarred by the battles we have fought, undaunted by the obstacles we have faced, and unburdened by the myths we were taught to believe.

Your commencement marks the beginnings of your acceptance of what Agee called "the terrific responsibility toward human life."

You now share that responsibility fully. You are adults. You are our peers. From today onward, you will shape your own lives and your own destinies.

And you will help shape our nation's destiny—and the world's. I ask you to give to your children a better world than we give to you. I ask you to temper your striving for material success, for the glitter of things, with the drive to overcome the injustice and misery that still stalk our nation and our planet.

I ask you to remember the words of the unknown poet, cited by Dr. Benjamin Mays:

> *I am only one*
> *But still I am one.*
> *I cannot do everything.*
> *But still I can do something.*
> *And because I cannot do everything*
> *I will not refuse to do the something*
> *I can do.*

To you, our children, our adult peers and partners in uncharted paths, we, your parents, say we are proud of you. We love you. And as you go down from this place, as you say farewell to your alma mater, be steadfast, be strong, be of good cheer, and may your dreams be your only boundaries henceforth, now, and forever.

VERNON E. JORDAN, JR.

Vernon E. Jordan, Jr., senior partner, Akin, Gump, Strauss, Hauer & Feld, prominent in the civil rights struggle in the sixties, president and chief executive officer of the Urban League, has become a singular voice of strength and knowledge about race in the United States.

In May of 1981, the founder of Delphinium Books was attending her son's graduation from the University of

Pennsylvania; the commencement speaker was Jordan, whose own daughter was graduating that day.

This essay, which originated as the commencement address for the class of '81, appeals to the humanity in all of us. It urges the graduates, and all those who hear these words, to use the same impulses, the same energy and enthusiasm that they are bringing to their personal careers to help those less fortunate.

Jordan brings an originality of idea to all the problems he tackles as lawyer, member of corporation boards, and appointee to government commissions.

TRIPS

TRIPS

David Michael Kaplan

E'RE DRIVING SOME-
WHERE IN A CAR, MY FATHER AND MOTHER AND
brother and me. We're going on a trip! To where I don't
know, but it doesn't really matter. Trips are wonderful. We
go someplace we've never been, and when we get there,
everything is different. Along the way, there are marvelous
sights to stop and see. My father would rather not, but he's
outnumbered here. My mother tells him it's educational for
my brother and me, but really, I suspect, she wants to see,
too. We have seen: The World's Largest Turtle Farm.
Yemanasee Indian Village. Our Nation's First Oil Well.
Cockatoo Jungle. The Hudson Miniature Train and Seashell
Museum. Santa's Workshop. The Monondaga Caverns. And
several zoos and monuments and battlegrounds. Even the
names of the towns we pass through—Drummond, Lady-
ville, Battersea, Spivey's Corners—sound like places in
fairy tales, and wonders are everywhere. At a gas station

once, the owner took us around back and showed us a row of glass cases, in each one a different spider or scorpion.

This trip will be a long one, I know, because my mother's overnight bag sits between my brother and me on the back seat of the old Packard; the trunk must already be full with our other suitcases. Putting it here also helps keep us from squabbling. He is four, still a baby; I am eight. On the front seat, my mother has a picnic basket from which she'll pull out bananas, tuna salad sandwiches, celery and carrot sticks. My father doesn't like to stop for lunch when we're on a trip—When I go, I like to go, he says. He would drive straight through if he could, stopping only for gas and oil and directions. And rest stops. He warns us to time these with the gas stops, but we often can't, not even my mother. When we stop, we'll get Cokes from long ice chests or—my favorite—grape Nehis. While my father chats with the attendant (there is no self-service yet, that is years away), I'll go to the rest room, a frightening, foul-smelling cave. My cousin has told me that little boys are often whisked away—and worse—in gas station rest rooms. I keep the door ajar and try to go fast.

At the end of the day, we'll stop for dinner, always at Howard Johnson's. My father plans each day's destination by Howard Johnson's.

They're clean, he says. You know what to expect.

The air, dry and grassy, swirls through the open windows of the car. It is hot, summer. My mother has opened the buttons of her dress so that when she turns I can see the cream-colored bra beneath. My brother and I are wearing shorts; the rough horsehair seats of the Packard make my legs itch. My father drives with one hand on the wheel, elbow out the window. Driving seems simple for him—he is masterful, confident. He will get us where we want to go. On the radio, the Four Rays are singing "You, My Love," a hit of the season. I've heard it so many times that I can sing along:

You, my love—
You are the one I dream of, love.
Let me hold you in my arms . . .

It is beautiful, I think—it's what love must be. I try to imagine being in love, but can only think of Patty Underhill, the quiet blond girl with dirty fingernails who sits near me in school. I decide I love her. I close my eyes; I am driving and Patty Underhill is beside me. We're going to Howard Johnson's and somewhere, somewhere, I don't know where, after that.

Barn, water tower, cows, my brother chants as we pass them. He's naming things a lot these days, and I find him boring and silly.

My father changes the radio station; the Four Rays vanish. He fiddles with the dial. I hear snatches of other songs, static, and then—a baseball game.

That's more like it, he says.

My mother sighs. She will tolerate this.

I don't know which teams are playing, but it doesn't matter. I'm just happy that the game is on, that my father is happy. There's something comforting in the drone of the announcer, the low hiss of the crowd that rises to a roar whenever they hit the ball. It's wonderful that somewhere men are playing baseball, and that here, many miles away, we can hear them.

I put my hand out the window, cupping it, then slowly unfolding it so that my fingers extend directly into the wind. I feel its pressure change on my hand; I pretend my hand's a sailboat. Cars whiz by with a snicking sound, like a pair of fast-closing scissors. I stare into their windows and glimpse families who look like us. Where are they all going? I'm amazed there are so many people on so many different trips. All across the country, there must be thousands of roads we aren't on, and cars with people inside I'll never see, and gas stations and restaurants with even more people inside sitting in booths, eating. It makes my head spin; it seems only God could keep track of them all.

I stick my head out the window and feel the wind, hot and tarry, against my face. It pulls hard at my lips, my cheek, and I have to keep my eyes closed. I can hear nothing but wind. And within the hollow that the wind makes, I hear my blood pulsing, and I think, I am alive.

Pull your head back in, my father tells me.

I do. But I still feel the blood in my temples, my skin tingling. I keep my eyes closed to listen to the wind within me, fainter now, like a seashell held up to my ear. The wind is telling me, You are different from anybody who's ever lived before.

And now I'm driving, not my father. The road is a turnpike, and the car is a slate-blue Corvair convertible, the first car I ever owned. I'm driving with the top down, the wind roaring in my ears. It's still summer, and the sun is almost blinding against the concrete. The Top 40 station plays "The Lonely Bull" or "The Girl from Ipanema" or "Cast Your Fate to the Wind," and I imagine Spain, islands, banana trees. I turn to a classical, then a country-western station—it doesn't really matter what the music is, it's all a soundtrack to my life, turning and soaring like the road itself in unexpected windings and vistas. My destination doesn't matter either; it's enough that I'm moving. The road's endlessness is wonderful, and I feel I could drive forever. As the car climbs a rise, I feel I'm flying; below me are treetops, a river, houses, a boy burning leaves. He glances up as I fly above, and leans against his rake. I imagine that he wishes he were me.

The radio plays "Gonna Find My Baby" by Bobby Blue and the Soul Men. I love this song. I turn it up louder and sing along with Bobby's smoky voice:

> *Hey, gonna find my baby,*
> *Oh yes, I will.*
> *Gonna find her tonight, right now . . .*

And now I know where I'm going—it's to see a woman. I'm in love! She lives miles away, in another city, and I often make the trip to see her. In the past month I've been dropping in on her unexpectedly. I tell myself I like surprising her, but I really do it because if I called, she might tell me not to come. It's been that way with us lately.

I don't think it's going to work, she's told me.

Why? Why do you say that?

It's just something I feel.

But you've got to be more *specific*.

How can I? It's just something I feel.

If you can't say, then you're not sure, really.

No—

No, you're not sure?

No—I—oh, I don't know!

I'll come over. We'll talk.

No—please don't—

But I do. As I drive, I imagine getting off at the exit for her street and going past the house she's rented for the summer. It will be early evening. She may be on the porch, her long bare feet propped against the railing, drinking a Tom Collins. Or she may be inside at the small hand loom she's bought; she's decided to learn weaving this summer. If she's there, she will be both glad and not glad to see me. Though she tells me it's not good to see one another, still she'll let me stay, out of habit or affection or a loneliness she can't admit. And later, we will argue again.

Or she may not be there at all. If she isn't, I'll go eat somewhere and come back again, and again, circling like an eagle, waiting. Sometimes I've waited until almost midnight, and then, not wanting to know more, have gotten back on the turnpike and made the trip home.

Is that it? I ask her on the phone. Some other guy?

No.

I came over last night. You weren't there.

You shouldn't have come.

I waited till almost midnight!

I was out with some friends. I got home late.

There is someone else, isn't there? That's what this is all about.

Don't you understand? It's us—it's just us.

And as I drive, I realize that the most perfect moment, the happiest time of all, is right now, just driving to see her. Nothing can be sweeter than this trip through the summer evening. She may be there, she may not be—either way, there will be difficulties. But right now, nothing has yet soured; everything is possible. Travelling between where I've come from and where she is, I'm happy.

I know it used to be here, I'm telling the woman beside me in the car. She's not the woman I took so many trips to see, but another. She is you.

What used to be? you ask.

I shake my head. I won't say.

We're taking our first long trip since we've been married, and we're excited, yet a little nervous. Driving together for days is something we've never done before. And we're hot: it's summer, the afternoons are muggy. In the distance, like a gradually swelling bruise, the sky is turning purplish-green. The air seems amber, phantomlike.

I want us to get a new car soon, you say. One with air conditioning.

Even though I'm quite fond of my Corvair and don't want to give it up at all, I say, Sure.

You lean your head against me, and I put my arm around your bare shoulder. I'm proud of you, proud of us, proud that we're taking this trip together.

I've driven some miles out of our way to show you Dinosaurland. That's not its name—it had no name—but that was what my brother and I called it. We saw it on a childhood trip—a row of dinosaurs rising unexpectedly from a field beside the road.

They must be some kind of exhibit, my mother said.

We turned around and stopped, and found they weren't an exhibit at all, but the hobby of a middle-aged man in thick, black-framed glasses which, by contrast to his green work overalls, made him look almost professorial. He repaired lawn mowers by trade, but loved dinosaurs and had built these minutely detailed, three-quarter-size models from chicken wire and papier-mâché.

Every day somebody drops by and asks about them, he said. I meet a lot of people that way.

He took us out into the field. My father snapped pictures of my brother on a brontosaurus' tail and me leaning against a tyrannosaurus' leg.

Sometimes I come out here at night, the man told me, and just sit. Sometimes they make a sound, like they wanted to get up and go.

Well, now they have, I think. We should have spotted them by now, and we haven't. Almost twenty years have passed since the afternoon we saw them, but it's still hard to believe that things that huge could have vanished.

Maybe they were on the other side of the road, I say to you.

What were?

The dinosaurs.

What?

Just some old guy's craziness. And I tell you about them.

Weird, you say.

We must've missed them. Maybe we should turn around.

Honey, we've got a long ways to drive yet. And we've got reservations at the motel.

But I'd really like you to see them, I say.

It's OK. I can imagine them.

No, I think. *You can't.*

You slide away from me and rest your head against the window. You curl your legs beneath you on the seat, much as my mother used to do. In the distance lightning snaps and rain falls in wispy veils. The skin on my arms tingles. You nod, your head droops, your jaw slackens.

I wish you could've seen them, I say.

But you're already snoring lightly, your face puffy in sleep. You're not interested at all. And suddenly I think, We have made a mistake. I want to stop the car and—what? Turn around? Drive us back? But I can't. We're expected somewhere; we have reservations.

And then I'm terrified I might steer us off the road, as if my hands were no longer mine, but those of a demon. I clutch the wheel, concentrating on the highway's yellow line, imagining it a rope that could tow us safely along. My eyes smart with sweat, and I blink to clear them. I breathe deeply, again, again—and the panic passes.

I love her, I tell myself. And then aloud: I love her.

You open your eyes. What's wrong? you ask. You said something.

Nothing. I had a bad dream.

But how can that be? you ask, yawning. I was the one asleep.

Another summer, another trip. We're quarrelling again, about what, I don't know, and the trip has hardly started. In the back seat, the boys are squabbling too—something about why one colored in the other's book.

Be quiet, I say. What does it matter?

But he colored it wrong! our six-year-old cries.

Look—I'm going to smack somebody.

Why does everything have to be so physical with you? you say.

Well, you settle them then, I reply. You glare at me.

Why don't you count license plates? you suggest to them.

That's stupid, our eight-year-old says.

Dad, says his brother, can you turn on the radio?

Let's have a little peace and quiet, OK? It's going to be a long trip.

You reach over and turn on the radio. A heavy metal band pounds out leaden chords.

Yay—Twisted Sister, my son says. His brother begins bouncing in his seat, just like an autistic child I once saw in a TV documentary. I turn the radio off. They groan.

You're so rigid, you tell me.

I think how different trips have become, how they're no

longer taken with any feeling of excitement, but rather with a sense of foreboding, with little anticipation and fewer hopes. We go because we have to, or because we should, or because it would be good for the kids, or for us. Yet every trip seems the same somehow—the roads, the rest stops, the scenery, all the same. On the interstates all the billboards that used to advertise wonders have been taken down. The gas stations no longer have ice chests or attendants who'll show us strange exhibits in back. There are no more towns even; everything has become an exit, a vacuum that promises nothing beyond its name.

Wherever we go, we are the same when we get there.

I turn the radio back on and twist the dial. I find a ball game.

I don't want to hear any crummy baseball game, the oldest boy complains.

Hey, I say, this is the great American game.

He sighs dramatically.

Really, you should listen to this, I say. I turn it up.

You hand the boys ice cream bars from the cooler.

They shouldn't be eating those now, I say. We'll be stopping for lunch soon.

We packed lunch, remember? *You* wanted to drive through.

You're right, I realize. That is what we'd planned.

The interstate flows by like water.

I'll have a sandwich, I say.

You hand me a tuna salad sandwich. The bread tastes stale. A thin splotch of blue-green mottles one crust.

Mold, I say. This bread's got mold on it.

Let me see.

Don't you watch for things?

I'll scrape it off, you say.

I don't want you to scrape it off, dammit!

I throw the sandwich out the window.

Ka-boom, one of the boys says. Particles of tuna fish speckle the back window.

You know, I'm tired of you, you say.

I don't reply.

You're so overbearing.

I say nothing.

Look, you say. What I want to know is this: are you going to be this way the whole trip? Because if you are, I don't want to go with you.

I brake, and pull the car off onto the emergency strip.

What are you doing? you ask.

I stop, lean across, and open the door on your side.

Why don't you just get out here then? I say.

Uh-oh, they're fighting again, my youngest son says.

You sit tensely, arms by your side.

Go on, I say. Get out.

I push you.

Stop it, you say.

Is this physical enough? I push you again. Is it?

You strike me on the arm, hard.

Stop it, stop it, my son cries.

We fumble, me trying to push you, you flailing at me.

Stop it! I hiss.

You stop. We're both breathing heavily. A tractor-trailer rolls by with a gust and a whoosh. The car trembles. I reach over—you flinch—and I close the door. In the back seat, my youngest son is whimpering.

Be quiet now, I tell him. It's over.

And now I'm sitting with you in the Howard Johnson's near where we lived. I've suggested we get together there for breakfast. I'm happy to see that Howard Johnson's hasn't changed much over the years; the waitresses wear the same green-and-orange-striped uniforms, the same saltwater taffy and Boston baked beans and clam chowder entice us by the cash register. The pieman still tempts Simple Simon with his wares, and Simon, mouth open in hunger or amazement, is always about to reach for them.

I'm leaving this morning on a trip. I'm moving to another city, on another coast. From our booth, I can see my Toyota loaded with boxes, a rented roof rack on top. The furniture we decided I'd keep has already been sent ahead.

Do you know where you'll be living? you ask. We're lingering over our coffee, almost reluctant—now that the time has come—to part.

No. I'll look for a place when I get there.

Just don't get one of those tacky places with a pool and communal hot tub.

Oh no, I laugh.

I mean—I'd feel sad thinking of you in one of those.

I don't think they even have them back East.

I reach for the check, but you shake your head. My treat, you say. You're the one leaving.

When we go out, the sunlight is blinding, even though it's still early in the day.

It's going to be hot on the freeways, you say.

A scorcher.

How far do you think you'll get today?

Maybe the New Mexico border.

Send us some postcards, OK? The boys'll be interested.

We'll keep in touch, I say.

We embrace fleetingly, almost like our first embrace years ago when we weren't really sure what was happening or where we were going.

I'm going to leave now, you say.

A wave, a smile. I watch as your car turns the corner and you are gone.

A miniature orange tree sits on the front seat of my Toyota. I don't know why I took it, and already I regret it. I check the pressure in each tire, clean the windshield and side-view mirror. I inspect the roof rack. I look at my watch. New Mexico is probably too far for today, I think. Deep in Arizona would be enough.

I get in the car and shove the orange tree further over so I can shift more easily. As I'm readjusting the rear-view mirror, a young family comes out of Howard Johnson's. They're all blond, all golden—a mother and father and two little girls. They could be archetypal Californians, but their license plate is from a distant state. They must be on vacation, I think. The father opens the rear door for his daughters and lightly smacks each one on her bottom—a ritual, it seems—as she climbs in. They shriek with delight. One little girl has trouble with her seat belt, so her mother leans over and adjusts it for her. Then her father gets in, fastens his belt, and adjusts the rear-view mirror, just as I did. His wife asks him something, and he nods, and then they both laugh, as do the little girls in the back seat, and I think, How beautiful you all are. How I wish I were going with you.

D A V I D   M I C H A E L   K A P L A N

The author recalls the idea of this story coming from a dream: a man was driving somewhere with all his earthly goods. He was dispossessed, exiled, wandering. He sees another family and cries out, "Oh, how beautiful you are. How I wish I were going with you." The man's crying out became the end of this story, and the rest of the story followed, the author working backward in time through other trips, to his childhood.

The author notes: "The story is about a man's loss of love and family. But it's also about the other loss of youthful dreams and innocence in the 'trip' through life. The loss is inevitable and perhaps necessary, but we regret it nonetheless. And it doesn't stop us from wistfully looking at that other family in that other car and wondering if anything would have been better going with them, instead of taking the trip we did."

Kaplan writes this from Chicago, where he teaches writing at Loyola University; he's a Pennsylvanian who has lived in many parts of the country. Viking-Penguin has published his first short story collection (Comfort).

TRAVELING LIGHT

TRAVELING LIGHT

Eileen McGuire

W E STOP AT AN ARCO STATION JUST NORTH OF THE GRAPEVINE TO LET the dog throw up. I sit on my heels next to the dumpster in back, fists crammed into my jacket pockets, as I watch the Peke's little barrel chest heave in and out. It's colder here than it's been in L.A.

When she's finished I lift her, one-handed, and tuck her in the crook of my arm. "Poor Pearl," I murmur, and she looks up at me with a confused expression in those bulging eyes. My knees are stiff from squatting in this chill. As we head back to the car I spot Gary's wide forehead over the top of the magazine rack in the snack shop. My sister Fran is still sprawled across the back seat of the Toyota, a quilt pulled up to her eyebrows, pretending to sleep.

She sits up when I open the car door.

"Baby OK?" she asks dreamily.

"It was that McRib sandwich you gave her."

Fran chuckles. "Sorry. Should have let Gary eat it." Fran is a gourmet cook with a fascination for the dark side of the culinary arts. One of her hobbies is buying the latest fast food and submitting it to dissection and analysis.

"Where is the boy wonder?" she asks.

"Reading magazines," I reply as I settle Pearl on the passenger seat. "Sherman, the boy wonder" is Fran's latest nickname for my boyfriend Gary. "I'd better get some gas quick. I'm getting worried about the time."

I pull the car around to the self-serve island and wrestle with the gas nozzle as Gary emerges from the shop and lopes over to join us.

"Guess who died?" I can see a new *Rolling Stone* under his arm.

"Buddy Holly," Fran says from the back seat.

"Ha, ha." Gary smirks at her. "No—Professor Long-hair. Remember that album I played for you, Brenda?"

I nod as I replace the gas cap and snap the cover shut.

"He was a seminal blues artist." This last sentence is for Fran's edification. She flops back into a horizontal position as Gary folds his long body into the front seat.

"Move over, Pearl." He shoos the dog into the back. "Your Auntie Fran wants to snuggle with you."

I check the oil. It's down a quart, so I open a can of Castrol from the kit I keep in the trunk.

As it glugs into the engine I dicker over whether to ask Gary to take the next stretch. He's blind as a bat at night. If we make Paso Robles by 10:30 we can reach Salinas by one A.M. Mom will be waiting up. The sooner we get there the sooner we can get to sleep, get an early start on tomorrow. When I slam the hood shut I have a straight-on view of Gary's tonsured crown through the yellow glare on the windshield. He's deep into the *Rolling Stone*, and I decide

I'm too jumpy to sleep anyway.

"Great review for the new Dylan," Gary tells me as I get in. He starts to read me the highlights as we cruise back onto Highway 5.

The plan is to drop Fran and Pearl off at my mother's in Salinas and head out, Gary and I, to Pacific Grove in the morning. Because I couldn't get more than four days off from my stupid job as a technical writer, we're already a day late for the workshop at Asilomar. It's one week of meditation practice with Vedi Prasand, whose spiritual method, The Path, we've been studying for the past six months.

Gary keeps the overhead light on and reads silently as we turn west on Route 46. Long, plaintive snores waft forward from the back seat—not Fran, but Pearl, whose truncated nose makes her breathe like a little bellows. Fran never snored in all the years we had to share the same bed; it was always the covers we fought over. Now that's the only thing on which Fran and Gary can agree—that I'm a "cover stealer." I deny it hotly, but I like it when the subject comes up. It's a relief that we can all laugh about something.

Fran appeared on our doorstep two months ago with a dourly handsome biologist named Peter Gibbs. They had run off together from their teaching jobs and marriages in Hawaii, which I figure is an incredibly boring place—how else could a man like Peter make a conquest of my big sister? His specialty is the moa, an extinct New Zealand bird that once stood taller than the ostrich.

They spent a week on my pull-out couch. Peter hardly spoke, and I feared he was making vicious judgments on us all. After he had flown back to the moa and his wife, I was quoted some of his choicer remarks: on Gary, "a wimp"; on my brother Bill, who had put them up in San Francisco, "a dope fiend"; and about me, "twenty-nine going on twelve."

His last words to Fran were, "Now you and your sister can sit around all weekend drinking coffee and talking about me." Which we did.

I didn't know what to do about Fran, except to give her a couch to lie on while she watched TV all day and worked her way through the half pound of killer weed Bill sent her. There was a trench in the couch now, a sculpture of Fran in negative space. I'd get home at a quarter to seven, just in time for reruns of "Hawaii Five-O," and find the three of them: Gary curled up on the floor writing one of his rock video reviews, Fran making cracks about McGarrett's greasy pompadour to Pearl. Half the time she wasn't speaking to Gary, who liked to ask her things like, "What do you see yourself doing in five years, Fran?"

Gary's version of what happened would end with a defensive "I was only trying to help." He'd purse his lips and study the back page of the sports section, covering the margins with his own penciled calculations of baseball box scores. "I let her watch what she wants," he liked to point out.

"Talk to me, Gary," I say. "I'm getting highway hypnosis."

He finishes a paragraph and tosses the magazine on the dash.

"OK. What do you want to talk about?"

"Aren't you nervous about Asilomar?"

"What's there to be nervous about?"

I knew he would say that. The fact that at this workshop we will decide whether to join Vedi Prasand for a year-long retreat devoted to The Path—that doesn't bother Gary. The big ideas never do.

There are things about The Path that worry me, like the idea that it was "dictated" to Vedi by an Indian saint who's been dead for three centuries. But the daily lessons have a way of lifting me up. Today, for example, our meditation is: "[Name a problem] is dissolving in light."

When I was growing up, there was God and sin, heaven and purgatory. Forgiveness was earned. You went to confession, did your penance, and for a minute, or a day, the slate was washed clean. On The Path there is no sin, only wrong thinking. Right thinking, in fact, is when you aren't thinking at all. Vedi says love is everywhere, like oxygen, free to everyone who learns to breathe it in.

I am ashamed to admit to anyone, even Gary, that sometimes when Vedi talks about unconditional love the first thing that comes into my mind is Pearl.

I sigh audibly, thinking of the dog.

"Is it Pearl again?" Gary says. "Don't make such an issue of it. How do you know they won't let you take her? They could have the retreat on a nice farm in New Mexico. Who's going to care if there's a dog around?"

"Vedi, that's who. Have you ever heard him say a good word about a pet? We're supposed to be releasing our attachments."

"Guru Nanak loved his elephant."

"That's symbolic and you know it."

"Bren, do your lesson." Gary smiles indulgently at me and massages the back of my neck for a few miles. He thinks he's more committed to The Path, since he started it first.

It was during one of the times we broke up—the third time, maybe?—when he heard Vedi on an early Sunday morning talk show and bought the book. First it was something neutral for us to discuss over the phone as we tried to "stay friends." Then Gary came over to show me the lessons, and I started using his book myself, though I could have gone to the Bodhi Tree and bought one of my own.

We dragged Fran off the couch one night and took her to one of Vedi's talks. She said she'd come just to see for herself what her kid sister was getting into. Vedi had a lot to impart that evening—three hours' worth—and it was pretty fascinating stuff, I thought: about his boyhood in Bengal, the right way to learn yoga (unavailable in America), the habits of tigers. Vedi could be fierce sometimes, in a way that made my stomach fold in on itself, but I had the sense that the full force of that presence could blast the everyday muck right out of a person, if it came to that.

He was uncharacteristically lighthearted and full of fun that night, I thought, hoping that Fran could appreciate the humor. He was even dressed casually, but with his usual elegance, in a silk shirt and ascot. The mostly female members of his inner circle sat at his feet (they always did, even if there were chairs available) and laughed hysterically at Vedi's stories.

"They look like nuns," was Fran's first comment as we stepped into the welcome bite of the night air.

I had to admit there was something about the women in Vedi's group—a scrubbed, self-righteous quality—that brought back our high school nuns.

"And what an old blowhard. He says, 'We didn't need toys in my day. We played with little sticks and cowpats.' Reminds me of Dad."

"Your father played with cowpats?" Gary said. Underneath the attempt at wit, I could tell he was aggravated by Fran's reaction to the talk.

"Dad used to look at our toys and tell us how he made do with a hoop that he rolled up and down the alley when he was a boy," Fran explained. "Must be that old windbag's appeal for you, Brenda."

That made me mad, too, so I said, "I figured that's what Peter's appeal was, Fran. The guy who despises the world, but thinks you're OK."

Fran didn't say a word all the way home. I felt guilty that I'd mentioned Peter. Gary was sulky, too. When we were getting ready for bed he said, "So what's my appeal?" I turned to him. There were creases forming between his brows and a bruised look in his eyes. After three years I knew this look—it presaged hours of mutual analysis that would end in his curling up in the hall with his sleeping bag to listen to all-night talk radio.

"I need to do my lesson," I said as sweetly as I could, and sat down cross-legged on my side of the bed to meditate. With my eyes closed I heard the closet door open and the swish of the sleeping bag as it slid off the shelf.

Now that Gary has turned off the overhead light I can pick out an occasional farmhouse or barn on the highway. The hills behind them are barely discernible, just black humps in the moonlight, dinosaur silhouettes.

The only music the radio can pull in on this deserted stretch is from a country station in Bakersfield. A tune fades into static and back again; I can just make it out. It sounds like Willie Nelson's ghost singing "Someone to Watch Over Me."

On another night, in a borrowed car, Gary and I traveled back from a rock concert at the Long Beach Arena on our third date. This album had just come out. He put it on the tape deck and I leaned back in my seat, letting those old songs, that voice, straight as an arrow, quaver in the air.

.   .   .

I felt so at ease with Gary, comfortable enough to allow the gaps in the conversation to widen, and let the music tell us what we wanted to hear. In front of my apartment Gary kissed me, lopsidedly, when we said goodnight.

I remember thinking, "This is it." Now I ask myself, "Was that me? Was that us?"

"[My doubts about Gary] are dissolving in light," I repeat to myself, as Pearl crawls into my lap from the back seat. In a moment there's a grinding sound from the engine, and my first thought is that the dog has somehow knocked us out of gear. We lose speed. When I press my foot on the gas pedal, nothing changes.

"Something's wrong. Gary, are you awake?"

"What is it?"

The oil pressure light pulses red on the dashboard. I pull the car onto the shoulder. Loose gravel pings off the sides as we lurch to a halt.

Fran uncovers her face. "Why are we stopping?" she moans.

"We're having car trouble, Fran," I snap at her.

Gary opens the glove compartment and starts rooting around for the owner's manual. I grab the flashlight, pop the hood release, and step out into a frosty stillness. My feet crunching on the gravel and a sizzling noise coming from the engine seem deafening by comparison.

Gary joins me as I peer under the hood. Everything, from the battery to the carburetor to the window-washing reservoir, is coated in shiny goo. I aim the light at the oil cap and take a sharp breath.

"Oh."

"Do you know what it is?" Gary asks.

I can barely say it. "I left the cap off when I put in the oil. Oh God, why did I do such a stupid thing?"

He puts an arm around me. One thing about Gary—he knows less about cars than I do, and he'll never rub it in.

"All right," he says. "Let's put more in and see what happens."

We don't mention the cause of the trouble to Fran, who's still bundled up, but upright, when we get back in. The engine turns over and we grind another mile or so before a final, sickening clunk shakes the car and stops us dead.

After a moment, Fran speaks.

"We're going to blow up. Can't we get to a gas station or something? Well, I'm getting out of here before this car explodes." She starts to fumble with the back of Gary's seat and we all get out. Pearl joyfully trots to the weeds at the edge of the shoulder and snuffles around for a place to pee.

"Why us? Why of all times, now?" I address the universe.

"Do you think life is trying to tell us something?" Gary says. I throw him a black look, which he doesn't notice in the dark.

"I think we should walk this way," I announce, pointing toward Paso Robles.

We stumble along for a quarter mile before there's a hint of a human dwelling. Fran isn't dressed for disaster—she has a green turtleneck pulled over pink cotton overalls and zories on her feet. The outfit suddenly infuriates me; and to think that I used to imitate slavishly everything this person wore, or said, or did fifteen years ago. Pearl irritates me too, wiggling uncooperatively under my arm, dying to wander off into the dark scrub at the side of the road. Then we'd have to waste a couple of hours calling for her while she hid in a bush three feet away, stubborn, secretive creature that she is. Gary's no help either, patting me on the back one minute and suggesting every other minute that we're going the wrong way.

His attitude toward The Path angers me in the same way. He hints at an understanding so deep I couldn't hope to comprehend it, then sees an ad for a rock writer in the classifieds and says, "Let's move to Portland instead."

After all these months doing the lessons, releasing my fear and resentment, here I am, in the crunch, right back at the bottom. Mad as hell.

"Lights," Gary calls back to us. "Up on the left."

Mike, the tow-truck driver, makes us all crowd in with him up front. "Regulations," he says, as his hoist with its "Jesus Saves" bumper sticker on the side tips my dead Toyota up forty-five degrees. As we speed across the seven miles to Paso Robles, he recommends a repair shop and a motel, then tells us about the other people he's rescued tonight. He likes his work.

A long sideburn like a daub of axle grease lines the fleshy cheek that's closest to me—very close, since I'm straddling the gear box. I've got both hands on Pearl's shoulders, and can feel her lunging forward to take a bite each time Mike's hand crosses to the gear shift. There's a crucifix hanging from the mirror and a package of chewing tobacco on the dash.

"Born-again Christian?" Gary asks.

"Said yes to Jesus on November 19, 1981."

"Got an anniversary coming up," Fran mutters from the other side of the cab.

"How did it happen?" Gary prods him.

"Long story—Gary, is it? Long story, Gary. Lord had me by the short hairs, so to speak. Hit me like a ton of bricks. Gave me back my peace of mind. Here's your station coming up on the right."

After we pull a few essentials out of the trunk of the Celica, Mike drives us three blocks along Spring Street, to the Willows Motel. He grins and waves and toots his horn as he flips a U-turn across four empty lanes and heads back toward the highway.

Inside we pool our change and send Gary down the hall for Tabs and cheesy peanut-butter crackers. I call Mom and tell her an optimistic version of the news. Fran rolls a joint on the nightstand and I fill an ashtray with water and set it on the floor for Pearl.

"No cable," I report as I page through the pitifully thin local TV guide. Gary and Fran are spreading crackers and bags of M & Ms on one of the beds. Gary takes the joint she offers him, though he usually refuses marijuana.

"Cheddar-flavored cheese food," Fran quotes from the back of a wrapper. "Look at that color. Wow."

"And beef jerky for Pearl," Gary says. "It's a party." He hands me the joint, smiling.

"You know what's on?" I say. "*Zhivago*." When I pull the knob that turns on the set, Omar Sharif is staggering through a snowy landscape. We pass the joint around again.

"A reader at the psychic fair last year told me that Pearl and I had a past lifetime together," I say. "I was dying in the snow, apparently. Pearl dragged me to safety."

Fran coughs out some smoke. "Yeah," she says. "I can see her with one of those airline brandy bottles hanging from her collar."

It's either the occasion or the dope, but the idea strikes us all so funny that we laugh until Pearl gets scared and barks. "Shhh," we hiss at her in unison, then crack up again.

I wipe tears from my eyes and gulp to catch my breath. Fran and I used to laugh like this. One summer Mom went back east to visit relatives and we had the house to ourselves, my brother Bill and Fran and I. Fran's future husband, Dave, would come to the door every day wearing a different disguise. I'd try to look even stranger when I answered the knock, just to break his concentration.

I was fourteen and trying to mold my frizzy hair into the smooth helmet shapes that were *de rigueur* in Salinas. Dave was one of the only members of the opposite sex I spoke to, except for Bill, whom Fran and I called "the boy" that year, and who didn't count.

Dave was going to make movies someday, and I would review them in national magazines. Bill thought he wanted to be a photographer, or a priest. Fran never said what she wanted, except that getting out of Salinas was an essential part of it.

If someone had asked me what I wanted most, and I told the truth, I'd have said "a boyfriend."

When we turn out the lights Gary reaches his hand out and I reach mine out and we hold hands as we fall asleep. He used to wrap himself around me as we slept, early on. I began to disentangle a leg and let it slide over to a cool, empty part of the sheet. Now I roll away until I end up next morning on the far edge, with all the covers.

I think of how it will be on the retreat: a small cabin, bare of furnishings, maybe a rag rug on the floor. We rise early and meditate together on the porch. The group meets, then we each have our work to do. Everybody likes dogs. There is no conflict; we live in harmony.

The only problem is, how to make the leap. If only I could be hit by a ton of bricks.

When morning comes it's not a party anymore. The mechanic says I need a new engine. We'll have to proceed by bus.

As we walk to the Paso Robles Inn to console ourselves with a big breakfast, we pass a small, blue and white Victorian set like a trophy in its sloping yard. Gary touches my arm and says, "Wouldn't it be nice to live here?" Smiling at each other, we elaborate on the daydream—nice neighbors, lots of room, a brass bed with a patchwork quilt.

"I'd build you a greenhouse," Gary says.

"*Live* in Paso Robles?" Fran scoffs. "You've got to be kidding." She walks on ahead.

At the restaurant we pick a big booth by the window. "My treat," I announce cheerfully. Gary orders the Cattleman's Special, and still has room for the last of my sausage and potatoes.

"A new record for the trencherman," Fran gibes from behind her cup of black coffee.

Gary makes a face at her and stabs another Little Link. I know the track she's on. His size thirteen feet come next.

"God knows you're eating for three," she says, "when you count the clodhoppers."

He chews silently, glancing at me from under his eyelashes. I shrug: so she's my sister—what can I do?

I buy my ticket first, then walk Pearl on a strip of grass that runs down the block by the Greyhound station. The Salinas bus, a local, isn't due until 10. I let the dog meander, since she's going to be stuffed in a duffel bag for a couple of hours on the bus. When we're almost back at the Greyhound driveway, Gary rushes up to me. His fists are clenched at his sides.

"I have to get some stuff out of your bag," he says. "I'm going back to L.A."

"What do you mean? The workshop . . ."

"This isn't worth it. It isn't meant to be."

The way I hear it, "this" just doesn't mean the trip, or the workshop. It's the two of us.

"What happened?" My breakfast changes position in my stomach.

He gave Fran his ticket to hold while he played a video game, Gary tells me, and now she claims she doesn't have it.

"We'll buy another one," I say.

"I don't have the money to spare."

He says that with unmistakable relish. Even as I recognize the scene, I am compelled to play it out.

Fran sits inside the station, reading a San Luis Obispo paper, with her zori-shod feet propped up on her suitcase. She doesn't look up.

"I don't have his blasted ticket. He must have dropped it."

"Will you look again?"

"I don't have it."

Back outside I plead with Gary, stressing the importance of the workshop, the retreat, the lesson for today: "I could have peace instead of this." A picture comes into my mind, of me on a bus, gliding past a desperate, waving figure on the side of the road. It's a very tall man with big feet and thinning hair. I look quickly at Gary, afraid for a minute he can read my mind.

He hangs his head and sighs until we see the northbound bus pull in. Then he stands.

"I guess I'll come," he says.

Bill meets us at the station in Salinas, an unexpected and slightly ominous development. He's been summoned from San Francisco to help Mom bring us to our senses—Fran teetering on the edge of a divorce and me on my way into "a cult." I can tell the responsibility weighs him down. His cheek is pasty white and damp against mine when we hug.

"One good thing to come out of this," he jokes as he offers around his hash pipe on the way back to the house. "I'm not the black sheep anymore. We all are."

"We're a flock, boy," Fran says.

"Gary," Bill says. "I scored some real nice window-pane acid."

"Do you have it on you?" Gary asks.

I've steeled myself against a speech from Mom, but she disarms me the instant I step in the door.

"You've got the world on your shoulders right now," she says softly as I give her a kiss. She looks smaller every time I see her.

All I can think of as we sit at the kitchen table is that we've got to get out of here, fast. Bill and Gary tuck into the cold cuts and potato salad, but I can only watch. Mom tries to tempt me with a plate of sourdough rolls.

"I pray for you every day," she says.

I try to explain to her about The Path, how it gives you the means to jettison that accumulation of junk you call yourself—send it into space like so much useless cargo. I have to stop myself before I get to the part about tossing the family baggage overboard.

"This retreat, Mom, will let us pare down to the essential truths. No attachments, no distractions."

"You're going to quit your jobs?"

Gary keeps his eyes studiously on his fork.

I think I have her there—the devout Catholic, on whose dresser is a three-foot-tall statue of the BVM.

"Vedi believes that when you're on the right course, God will provide for you." I substitute "God" in the right place where I would normally say "the universe" or "life."

"You can't live on prayers," Mom says.

"Good potato salad. Good ham," Bill interjects helpfully.

"I got some sausage in for your breakfast, too," Mom says. She looks longingly at Gary. She loves a visit from a big eater.

He looks tempted. I give him a kick under the table.

"No, Mrs. O'Boyle. We're expected at the workshop."

"We're late as it is," I add, getting up. "Bill can drive us."

As we back out of the driveway, Fran holds Pearl like a teddy bear against her chest in the doorway, waving one paw goodbye.

"Don't drink the Kool-Aid," she calls out.

Asilomar is a camp for grown-ups, all dunes and pine needles, with conference rooms named "Sequoia" and "Cypress." It's toward Sequoia that we're headed now, uphill and at double-time, as if that would make up for our tardy arrival. Up ahead I can make out clumps of people; the morning session is breaking up. Vedi Prasand, in gold tunic and white pants, his bald head gleaming like polished wood in the sun, is leading a group down the walk toward us. He stops about five feet from us and folds his arms across his chest. A fawn-colored cashmere shawl falls like an exquisite beach towel from the crook of his arm.

His assistant says, "Gary, you made it! You're here!"

We'd left her a message early this morning. I'm here too, I'd like to point out, and I'm the one who got him here.

Vedi shakes his head slowly. "You'll never make up what you've missed. Never."

My heartbeat accelerates. Gary reaches out his hand and touches the shawl. "Vedi, didn't they tell you?" he says jocularly. "We had terrible car trouble. The engine blew up."

"Don't give me your excuses," Vedi says.

He casts a challenging look my way. I begin to wonder if I am not ultimately responsible for burning up my engine. Perhaps that part of myself that doesn't want to change was the force that undermined this trip.

"We're here now, Vedi," I hear myself answering him.

"Delia will give you the tapes," he says more softly, and we fall in with the others as he moves on.

A raga hums on the sound system in Sequoia as the group sits quiet before the evening session. Someone behind us has taken off his shoes and a potent odor of dirty feet does battle with the lesson in my consciousness. When we come to order, one of Vedi's assistants announces that seven people from the group at large will be chosen for a special committee. The committee of seven will choose the site for the upcoming retreat.

I'm excited and surprised when Gary is picked as one of The Seven. I try to catch his eye as he stands solemnly with the others, but he's too nervous or shocked to look back at me. The new committee leaves for a private meeting outside.

Vedi speaks for a half hour about seriousness, and the inner voice. One by one we have to come up to the front, sit next to Vedi, and make a speech about our own state of seriousness, or lack of it. The first couple of people are so scared they break down and cry, and Vedi holds their hands while they croak out a few sentences. This opens the floodgates for the rest of the audience.

I'm no better when I get up there. The most I can say for myself is that I weep quietly in public. Vedi's hand holds mine in a strong, dry grip.

I don't know if I'm serious enough, I say, whispering into the microphone. They're taping the session.

The right choice is the only choice, the inevitable choice, Vedi says. He pulls a Kleenex from a box on his lap with a flourish, and hands it to me. The group laughs, and I, too, find myself smiling foolishly as I return to my seat.

I feel so light you could tie a string around me and float me over the dunes. Funny, I don't like this disembodied feeling. My palm smells of sandalwood when I reach up to wipe another tear from my eye. Tomorrow, Vedi says, he will ask everyone for a final commitment to the one-year retreat.

Gary and I take a walk on the beach after our meetings. We're too keyed up to sleep. He's full of inside information: an Indian reservation in New Mexico is still the first choice for a site, and the second—isn't it perfect, he says—is a ranch outside of Paso Robles. The inner circle made lists of who they thought were the most serious people.

"I made three lists," Gary says.

We sit down on a piece of driftwood. Noxious, invigorating smells of rotting seaweed and fish remind me that it's Monterey coast we're sitting on. It's cold and there's only a hint of a moon. I lean against his shoulder.

"So I guess you've made your decision," I say.

"I guess Vedi's made it for me."

"I can't see how I'll ever sleep tonight." I burrow closer to him.

"Brenda," Gary says. "It's simple. You've got to make a choice. Look, I know—let's flip a coin."

"Gary, no. This is serious."

"All the more reason."

He digs a quarter from the pocket of his jeans. "Call," he says.

Tails is what I usually pick for the thing I want.

"Heads I go on the retreat," I say finally.

The coin tumbles up from Gary's fingers. He catches it with a slap. We squint at his palm in the moonlight. There's a face on the coin.

Gary hugs me. "We're going, sweetie," he says. "Aren't you excited?"

I feel raw and emptied out. I let the wind whip through me, like there's nothing there to stop it. My teeth begin to chatter. Is this what it's like, I wonder, getting down to the essence of your being? I am here in this new place, at the end of this long day, without anything I started out with—no car, no sister, no dog. Just Gary.

"I guess this is it," I say, trying to smile back at him, but the smile cracks and my voice breaks into a sob. I bury my face in his shoulder and cry.

"What is it, honey?" Gary says. "Did you get an insight?"

My cheek is gritty with sand from his jacket when I lift up my head. "It's Pearl," I choke out. "I miss her already."

E I L E E N   M c G U I R E

Since we selected this story for our collection, Eileen McGuire won a prize in the Raymond Carver Short Story contest, making us especially happy to be among the first to publish her work.

She writes about California with a sly sense of humor and a sympathy for people caught in the contradictions of contemporary life. Like the other authors in this collection, she has captured an authentic native voice.

IN THE BUS

IN THE BUS

Grace Paley

Somewhere between Greenfield and Holyoke
snow became rain
and a child passed through me

As a person moves through mist
as the moon moves through
a dense cloud at night
as though I were cloud or mist
a child passed through me

On the highway that lies
across miles of stubble
and tobacco barns   our bus speeding
speeding disordered the slanty rain
and a girl with no name   naked
wearing the last nakedness of
childhood   breathed in me
     once   no
     two breaths
a sigh   she whispered   Hey you
begin again
     Again?
again   again   you'll see
it's easy   begin again   long ago

FOR DANNY

FOR DANNY

Grace Paley

My son enters the classroom
There are thirty-two children waiting for him
He dreams that he will teach them to read
His arms are full of alphabets   some are strange
    even to him

Because of his nature
his fingers are flowers
Here is a rose he says   look   it grew right
out of the letter R

They like that idea very much   they lean forward
So   he says   now spell garden
They write it correctly in their notebooks maybe
    because the word rose is in it
My son is happy

Now spell sky
For this simple word the children
turn their eyes down and away   doesn't he know
the city has been quarreling with the sky all of their lives

Well he says spell home   he's a little frightened
    to ask this of them   What?
They laugh   They can't hear him say

what's so funny?   they jump
up out of their seats laughing

My son says hopefully   it's three o'clock
but they don't want to leave   where will they go?
they want to stay right here in the classroom they probably
want to spell garden again   they want to examine his hand

G R A C E   P A L E Y

*Grace Paley has written three of the most remarkable
short story collections of our time,* The Little Disturbances
of Man, Enormous Changes at the Last Minute, *and* Later
the Same Day, *the latter two published by Farrar, Straus
& Giroux. She can show us universality in the simplest
moments of human experience, and her simplicity is often
her sophistication.*

*Throughout her career, she has written poetry. A
book of her poems,* Leaning Forward, *was published by
the Granite Press of Penobscot, Maine, in 1985. She
has continued to write poetry, and we present recent
examples.*

*She has just ended a two-year term as the State
Author of New York, after receiving the Edith Wharton
Award. (Another of our contributors, E. L. Doctorow,
has succeeded her as State Author.)*

FRIDAY SUPPER

FRIDAY SUPPER

Joseph Papaleo

SARFATTI'S TELEPHONE VOICE RAN THROUGH HIS HEAD LIKE A MEMORY itself, the way memory brings back bits of conversation silently inside the mind and the same way he had been hearing voices most of the year, phrases in Neapolitan dialect as he was about to reach for a second pastry or even jaywalk into a street.

Sarfatti's voice echoed a mellow mood—philosophical, speaking out of reflection, saying to him, "Anthony, listen to me, please. I am saying *yes*, it *is* all right to change your name legally. It is *not* an insult to the people of your personal past, of the people who produced you and so forth—all those grandmothers and fathers from Naples—you know what I am trying to say?"

"Not from Naples. Most of my people come from Calabria, as a matter of fact," Anthony said and wrote on his desk pad.

"All right, then, they're from Calabria or Sicilia or Upper Swabia—it's all the same, don't you see what I'm telling you? It's a nice heritage we saw for a moment in *time*. And it got buried under another one, a new one, a hip one. And that's the train we happen to be on. You know what I'm trying to explain? I am saying it is only history. History. And I am saying this is America's age. Right now. Rome had its day and then the English were the lords of it all and the Germans had their days and the rest of them; they all had their day. So now it's America, and we happen to be Americans. A happy accident of history. And everybody in the world is trying to get on the bandwagon. My cousins in Italy ask me to send them the L.L. Bean catalogue and Timberland shoes. They know trout streams in the Catskills I never heard of—"

Anthony stopped the flow with his own enjoyment, "All right, Jack. Now listen to my question. I want to ask you this. How come you're still Jack Sarfatti? Why aren't you Jack Sarfield yet or Jack Smithfield? Why isn't your name Jack Smithfield?"

Anthony was smiling.

"Come on, Anthony, will you not make issues where none exist?" Jack's voice was losing the thin edge of respect he usually kept for his boss, as he went on talking, "So nobody in my family got around to it. That's all it was. But one more thing—nobody in my family ever got to be a vice president of a big corporation. You'll be giving seminars and speeches in Phoenix, and they will introduce you from the platform. A name change becomes simply a very practical thing. Like making a ledger that people can read very clear. You simply become Anthony Collins, and you get straight to the point. You don't ever have to give them diction lessons and spelling help. No more explaining to people that the *ci* in

Collucci is pronounced like the *ch* in choo-choo. You know what I'm saying here? And the first minute you have to spell it out, you lose half the audience—or somebody mispronounces it—right away people think, a weirdo from someplace foreign. And your own people who can't pronounce your name right—they get pissed off at you for having that unpronounceable name—that makes them seem stupid. They don't forgive that."

"All right, all right, you win." Anthony's hand was raised, but he was alone in his office. Jack, of course, could not see him. It was not even ten o'clock in the morning. "Jack, I love you," Anthony said. "I pray that I can be sure of everything in the world like you are. But right now I can't even identify the feelings I have. Is it embarrassment? Betrayal, the way you say? Why do I feel so uneasy?"

Anthony heard only silence in the wires and spoke again, "But listen, Jack, don't think for a minute I don't appreciate your input. I really like what you say. Thanks for being a real *paesan'*. Why the hell is this thing giving me so much trouble?"

Jack laughed. "Trouble. All right, don't worry, be happy. And I want you to know right now that even after you change your name, you still get permission to use ten dialect words a day. Like *gavon* and *Maron* and *strunz'* and *fongool*. Do you *gabeesh* me?"

"That's enough. I *gabeesh* I got work to do. I have to leave the office early. Tonight's my supper with the family."

"But you said you would have a drink with me and listen to my presentation I'm going to make out there."

"Jack, right after supper—about nine—I will be hitting you for free drinks. You can read it to me. I'm never long down in the Bronx. I couldn't survive it."

Anthony put the speaker down and went back to his

desk. The rest of the day passed without meetings, and by five he was deep in his papers, having lost track of time. Denise came in to remind him—time to go to the Bronx.

To his secretary, Denise, a Westchester man of Anthony's position still eating with his folks in the Bronx was erotic. It made her think of the big weddings in the olden days and Anthony as the vanguard of a new man, a new hope, a man-fan of white lace and bridal shops and gift-filled showers. She watched him get his jacket, pack his case, and leave, with a sense of awe.

Fifteen minutes later he was stuck in a line of stopped cars on the Bronx River Parkway. He knew it was like this every Friday night, but he always raced out of the garage under the offices and went straight for the nearby parkway entrance that took him to this same spot where he always waited bumper-to-bumper.

He saw, the edges of his eyes, the park paths along the river and a small waterfall that came through white birches and paths that led nowhere into green foliage—a place he had always intended to come to and explore on a Sunday.

The look of stillness at this spot always attracted him and held him back at the same time. He could not explain it, but he felt the double pull every time. It was the place where he first began remembering his dream, first like pictures, like snapshots that appeared and got bright only a moment before going dark.

It was the same dream: inner pieces of his rear molars were sloughing off, falling down like a shore of soil after heavy rains. Like silver fillings that had lost their molecular strength, they fell in pasty chunks between his thumb and index finger, and as he probed his mouth, they turned into gray, silvery sand. Then he awoke, startled.

It was such a vivid dream that he would always check his teeth right away and be surprised that there were no spaces.

Ironically, his actual teeth *had* been getting bad; Steinfeld, the dentist he trusted his mouth to every six months, sent him to a periodontist, who was young and super-confident and who wove a story of decaying gums reabsorbing themselves into nothingness. But he nodded for Anthony, one of the lucky ones, because many come in with gums that are impossible to save.

Impossible to save held inside his head like an echo. Last night he had called his internist about waking in the middle of the night in a sweat and finally thinking it might not be the dream. "Yes," the doctor's voice said, "it could have been something to do with the heart. But you had no pain, no numbness, none of the symptoms to worry about. And it also could have been your hypertension, but nobody will ever know how to diagnose that as long as you are obese. I've told you that for a long time now. But why not try some Tenormin at night. Another fifty milligrams before you turn in."

Anthony came out of the reverie, shaking his head while he watched a man who had appeared near the waterfall with a black-and-white dog. The man and the dog walked under the birches, caught in patterns of light and shade. Then Anthony lost the two of them as the cars in front of him moved, and he had to join the speeding line.

But as the car accelerated, he felt another dream, something more recent, closer than the teeth—June, the air seemed just like June—he was a child—he looked eight or nine. He was also his present self walking at the side of this child.

He knew without words the child-fears inside the child, looking now for its home street, lost in its own neighborhood.

He was going up the steps of the old house near Arthur Avenue; he had just arrived to find the family already seated for dinner—Sunday. He announced to them all that he was *going on a diet:* he had heard the phrase somewhere.

They were laughing at him, and his mother was talking to him in Italian. She was saying *let's see, let's see if you can do it.*

And one other glimpse: he was sitting in a chair in a bedroom, and the voices of the family downstairs could be heard having a holiday party. He faced the sunlight slanting in through the windows and was about to weep, lost again in the upstairs.

Now he saw that this was part of even more dreams, of many. The traffic moved and drew him away from reflection; he began passing cars through the narrow lanes along Bronxville and by Mount Vernon and the city line was ahead of the pack and coming too fast to make the Gun Hill Road exit.

But he made it, with great brake squeals, bouncing up the exit ramp and almost into an old couple in a vintage light blue Dart. He watched their lips move silently a short stopped time before passing them and accelerating along Gun Hill Road eastward, very far east, to the new house, which he called *the great compromise*—not exactly total escape from the Bronx and the new Jamaicans but far enough east to see only a few of them.

The neighborhood was essentially Jamaican now. And Anthony's father liked them: they were neat about their houses and their clothes. They were always fixing things. It was this aura of industry about them that made his immigrant mind happy and calm; they must have virtue.

Still, the old man would look down the streets and say, "But it all happens too fast. I don't deny any man his house, but where is my world?"

"Yonkers," Anthony would reply, but his father would ignore the son for interrupting his poetry.

His mother was concerned with magic stories, wherever they might be, underneath the surface. The new immigrants, the ones they hear about from the ancient islands and forgotten hills, now housed illegally in Queens—they brought new magic.

Anthony stopped his thought train; he was actually listing the agenda for tonight's supper conversation and starting to do all the voices. It was Friday, all right—linguini and clams and mussels and shrimp (if you can get them real fresh) and sometimes squid, if not frozen, and a vegetable, a salad, followed by a large argument for dessert.

And during the meal someone would surely say, "You know what I got the *woolies* for these days? Some nice, old-fashioned squid with the raisins and the anchovies and pine nut sauce. Remember that dish from the olden days?"

And then another, as the fish plates were being put down, would mention again that you really didn't have to eat fish on Fridays anymore if you didn't want to, though a lot of people still stick to it out of respect.

He could actually make tapes and send them by messenger on those Fridays when he was out of town on business.

The house now appeared, and he parked in front and

walked up the path between the small grass lawns on either side. A new pink flamingo, a steel rod in its middle, stuck up from the grass on the right lawn.

He found his father waiting at the open front door. Anthony pointed back to the flamingo and shook his head.

"What do you want me to do?" his father said. "Last week the new neighbor, Mr. Kelley, he brought it to me. I think you met him, too, the day you was here he was looking."

The old man watched his son's face; it always held his wife's knotted, light fury in it. He spoke to mollify it, "So what I'm supposed to tell him? I'm sorry, Kelley, but I can't take no flamingo because my son Anthony, he's with the big corporation now, they put his picture in the paper last month, and he thinks pink birds is tacky. So I can't accept. Anthony, this man had it gift-wrapped special for me; he carried it from Florida just for me—by hand. Come *on*."

Anthony walked through the door toward the kitchen, his father in pursuit. At the kitchen door, Anthony said to him, "I just got a great idea. Now you give *him* a black jockey holding the brass ring—for *his* lawn."

His father smiled but did not answer. His mother looked up from the stove, "I just heard the both of you. Anthony, don't tell me you don't know what is *mala figura*. It's looking bad in front of others. You have to accept a thing like that or it makes a bad impression. But where you been so late?"

"It's the Bronx River Parkway. They won't change it and the traffic is ten times more—"

" 'How long could it take from White Plains,' I'm saying to myself. And then I'm saying 'God forbid anything happened to him.' "

"Mom, they haven't changed that parkway in sixty

years—so five o'clock comes, and it's a parking lot."

"Well, I say thank God there's something in this country they don't change every five years." His mother held up her right hand.

Anthony turned to his father and nodded; the first salvo had been fired. His father sank into his kitchen chair (with pillow only for him) and said nothing. Retirement had shrunk him to the size of the kitchen.

Anthony was overcome by it often; he did not like his father becoming miniaturized because his mother had so much energy left while his father contemplated retirement, which he regarded as a prelude to burial. "Pop," he said, "you been thinking about my offer? Take a fast trip down to Florida. Stay a while, look around. Feel out the rhythms. Give it a try. Then buy what you want, and I'll assume the mortgage. Or just rent something, and I'll take care of the rent—and you can come back up here whenever you want. And when you want some company, I'll fly down a weekend."

His father's tone became whiney, "You know, my dear son, in *my* time, in *my* years, I made my moves in the world. I even came here from the old country with five cents in my pocket, and I worked from the day I got off the boat. Then I lived Brooklyn, Grand Street, Arthur Avenue, and out here. Don't tell me you forgot my journey?"

Parts of it, in some way, sounded false to Anthony, a story much too old to be true, much too familiar not to be constructed from the typical, like a movie that starts as if new and then gets stale without anybody knowing how.

All right, the new movie was still Florida, where Fusco had gone to thrive in Orlando (before they built Disney) with a big Sunoco station even larger than anything he had on Southern Boulevard.

Anthony now brought up Fusco, and then Zambetti

the contractor, re-energized in Hallendale, and the Colosimo's, with two stores going strong in Naples, and even little Di Nome, the Allstate agent with a bad heart doing great down there.

But the old man said, "All right, I will move down when you move down. All right?"

Anthony answered quickly, "But you can go right now, and I wish I could. I need to stay at corporate headquarters a few more years. There's more to come."

He saw his father's head nodding, sinking a little, the miniaturized look. "But Pop, I'll be down—I'll come most weekends, I'll talk to you every day. We'll have lots of time together."

Mrs. Collucci had begun putting food on the long table: artichokes stuffed with breadcrumbs and parsley and garlic chips, peppers in oil, linguini with shellfish, and two pans of fish fillets with a tomato and caper sauce on them.

"Where's Ralph and the kids?" Anthony said.

His mother shook her head while she studied the table, "Your older brother, for a change, is late. The only man who gets lost in Massapequa when it's time to come over here. You didn't hear that—he needs a radar for Christmas. He called and said start without them. Call your sister upstairs."

Anthony went to the bottom of the staircase and called his sister's name and came back to sit next to his father. "Pop, I just can't help feeling that you would like Florida. Even more than escaping the winters. Your whole gang's down there. You should give it a try, too. See just what it is."

His mother's head leaned close to him as she lowered a basket of sliced bread on to the tablecloth, "Anthony, listen to me a minute." Her voice was low and tight. "I am hearing many things about down there, you know what I'm saying. Like the water. And things *in* the water. Some say one day all the water down there will be bad. Then you can't cook, you can't wash without bottles. To make a cup of coffee you go buy a bottle of water first. You want that? And the new people down there who come off the mountains from Cuba, from Peru, from Salvatore—they have germs inside them from when they was born that don't kill them. But once it touches us, it kills. We have no resistance. Like what they brought in, the AIDS. They brought that, you know. That came in from Florida."

Anthony held back and began to eat very fast, using his fork to go after food in the serving plates. His mother straightened up and kept her stare on him for response.

He nodded to her as he filled his mouth. "All right," he said. "And what makes you think we don't have people like that up here, too?"

"Yes, but up here I know how to handle them. I got ways to ward them off. I can keep them away from here. Though I heard in the hospitals downtown where they have their babies—born with diseases they don't even know what they are yet. Babies who look like monsters. Germ babies who are green when they give birth. Babies with two tongues. And do they bury these babies? No. They hand them to the mothers and let them go down to the streets like the rats in the tunnels and the subways."

It was the alligators-in-the-sewers story again, a new variant. Anthony was losing control and put his fork down on the tablecloth, about to speak when his mother turned back to the pots still on the stove. A voice came into the pause, "And don't think that's so crazy, my brother."

It was Catherine, come from her room, knowing she was older and always speaking to Anthony as if she were wiser. She knew he was about to explode and tried to stop him. "Anthony, this is real stuff," she said. "These people come from the primitive countries with germs our science never heard of—and have lived with these germs thousands of years. Like the Bangla Desh."

She said the name like an incantation and then shook her head for her brother's stolid face, "Just read the magazines," she said to him. "These germs are killing us off like flies. Because we *don't* live in that particular dirt and squalor."

"All right," Anthony said with mock calm. "Please tell me how does dirt and squalor protect people from disease?"

"Because, my little brother—" Catherine came round the table and sat across from him, "because *this*." She pointed a finger at him over the food. "The filth they live in is their salvation. It kills off a lot of them when they have babies. The ones that survive are immune, and they can come here and kill us just by sneezing in our face."

"Is this out of the *New England Journal of Medicine* or the 'National Enquirer'? Which medical journal do you read? Tell me, do these people also walk the night? And do they glow in the dark?"

His sister turned her face away from him and took an artichoke, eating it leaf by leaf, biting and scraping to expel anger, and finally said, "Once upon a time you used to believe us."

"I know," Anthony said. "And I'll be sorry when one morning I wake up and find my teeth falling out."

Anthony stopped; he was suddenly in collision with memory. He tried to make connections. But his sister's voice kept talking to him, "You know when you'll finally be satisfied? When the crazies come and get you, and you're full of blisters and too weak to move—"

Anthony remained silent, his face losing expression. His mother noticed quickly, "You feel all right? Catey, look at that white face on him. I could tell something was wrong with him the minute he walked in here tonight. Go get the thermometer."

Mr. Collucci, who always strove for continuance, stood up and leaned over the steaming bowl of linguini, "Come on, let's eat first," he called out. *"Bon appetito* now and talk later."

He began serving with the big steel spoon and fork, Anthony first, then the others. "Come on, it's Prince Spaghetti day; you got to dig in."

Catherine smiled at her father's reference to the old commercial and his incongruous, new, slangy phrases. Anthony looked down at his plate, and Catherine asked him, "Did I say something to offend you? I didn't intend it, you know."

Anthony looked up from his food, "No, Catey, not at all. I just made some kind of connection—which stuck in my head when you just said something. Some word? I don't remember what it is. I couldn't remember—"

His sister said, "Oh, that happens to me—I'll hear a word, and it will lodge in my head like a rock, and I can't see around it, like—"

Anthony was nodding at the picture; their father smiled at the amity. Mrs. Collucci was leaning over her final pot, and they watched her flourish as she poured its steaming water into the sink, then came up with the asparagus, which she slid quickly onto a serving plate.

Catherine had been chopping garlic buds, holding the slices in a small dish while her mother covered the asparagus with olive oil from the copper pouring can made in Naples seventy years ago. Then Catherine sprinkled the garlic slices over the plate, and her mother squeezed a lemon over it all. "This is the Spring," Mr. Collucci said. "God says, see, I am still magic for you. I make this again out of nothing."

"God. Just him, God," his wife said. "Who can't find his way to Mass even on Easter."

Anthony accepted the first plate again but waited for his mother to sit. She seemed happy to see them all and pleased with the fresh asparagus, yet began talking instead about dope addicts who were pregnant and shooting cops in Queens and giving birth in jails, making a Bronx Breughel of this potential army of babies and drugged mothers about to rush upon the full-grown Italians.

Then she went into rough sex, a new and more mysterious horror: boyfriends strangled their dates during this seizure, though Mrs. Collucci knew the TV didn't tell about a lot more that was worse. "It must be too *kinky*," she said, using another of her new words learned from the children, this one for describing not only slum monsters but also mayors and ministers and congressmen and all the others we used to think were people to look up to—better people.

She was interrupted by the arrival of her first son and his family. The attention turned to little Mark and Marie. Anthony now made his regrets, citing night business meetings, knowing his mother would now lecture on overwork and its dangers as described on the six o'clock news. The sin called STRESS.

He watched her get up and start for the kitchen, but Catherine had anticipated her and already had the large weekly brown bag for Anthony.

Mrs. Collucci took the bag and said, "It's only a few chops, some leftover pasta and fish, you better eat this right away for the fish, and a little prosciutto we had twice already and it's almost a pound left. You could put it in a light sauce with a little tomato, you could have with a little mozzarell'— I put some provolone in, too, because it goes good with that."

It helped him ease out of the house on smiles, and his own smile was still stuck on his face when he reached the parkway entrance alone with the brown bag on the passenger seat next to him. His last picture of the house held—his father turning away as Anthony said the final good-bye, as if his father were trapped in there and now abandoned.

But now they would all sit and say things about his excessive work, his neglect of family, and eventually settle down while Catey read the astrology page aloud. By TV watching time they would have forgotten his rudeness.

When he reached his apartment, the White Plains streets were quiet, enough to make a nice slowdown inside him. He walked up the steps to his apartment house instead of taking the elevator. Once inside his door he went to make coffee, after dropping the brown bag on the bottom shelf of the fridge; it took the entire shelf and pushed up the wire rack above it.

He gained back his own rhythm by watching the coffee drip down, then took a cup with him to the living room as he took off his jacket.

This cup of hot coffee and the couch and the TV remote box was his expurgation. He pressed buttons and went through all the stations: fights, chases, stabbings, blood spurting from rolling eyes, creatures spewing forth sticky goo from holes inside them, human faces melting into molten puddles, a knife with its own brain chasing a woman down a dark street in green shadows, and finally an advertisement for the eleven o'clock news and the real-life horrors coming up.

He tapped off the sound and picked up the evening paper as the phone rang. Jack's voice was talking to him, "So I am still waiting for you down at Oliver's."

"All right," Anthony said. "I am just recuperating

from supper. I just realized my mother and sister get all their facts on what is going in the world from the TV news."

"So we all have hallucinations. Tony, believe me, *I know* what you feel right now. I know how it works on the head. I call my father's house the echo chamber. I hear the same words every time I go there, the *same words*, do you understand me? Followed later by the Greek chorus—so you forgot your mother's birthday, your father's name day, your sister's anniversary, your niece's christening, your brother's saint's day. And whatsa matter you stay away; you must love your job more than you love your mother, your father, your brother, your sister, your grandfather's memory, your niece, just fill in the blanks. Want me to go on?"

"Only if you want to hear a man puke over the phone."

"Then come on down here, Tony. I got a little surprise for you that popped into Oliver's and is looking for an active evening, eyes tight, under the sheets. So don't start pining again for that woman."

Anthony was smiling. "No pining. I'm in a new stage. Patching. I'm patching."

"Good. Then come and get your band-aids. Come and meet Miss Reality. Come on."

"Great, and start the same thing over again? I got to take it easy."

"Nobody in this place wants to get married tonight, Tony. I swear it. Just a little doobie doobie do. Don't you *gabeesh*? Come on, don't be an asshole. You broke up eight months ago. I got two nice people down here. I'm buying the drinks—"

"I'll try. But if I don't show in an hour, you'll know I fell apart." He put the phone down fast, before Jack could answer, and walked to the bedroom where something made him turn down the bedspread neatly before washing up and putting on his jeans and corduroy jacket.

He looked at the bed; the woman cleaned on Friday, and the bed always looked especially neat, composed, inviting. He began to think of Beth in that bed; she had ordained the going into it and the going out of it from irrational reasoning he still could not fathom.

He was ready to leave but went to the bathroom to brush his teeth and then put some holding fizz on his hair. As he put the can in the cabinet he saw the box of condoms and stared at it a few seconds before taking a packet for his wallet; he was embarrassed.

He went to the outer door and switched off the lights and stood in the darkness a minute or two. He was sweating again. It came from bad planning. He must rearrange Friday nights and always have some people he liked to see after the supper with the folks, some quick icy minds like Jack's.

He closed the outer door and walked to the elevator. The trip down was quick and his walk less than a block. Jack was talking with two women when he walked in. Both had black hair and the one on his left a shapely thin body, while the other was shapely but heavy.

Their hands moved in familiar ways as they spoke. "Here's my buddy coming right now," he heard Jack say, and both women turned to him as he came up to the bar.

He put out his hand; the woman nearest him, the thin one, nodded at his hand and then looked into his eyes. "I'm Denise," she said. "We were just about to give you up. I though he was making believe."

"Well, Jack sometimes thinks I *am* invisible in this world," Anthony said, and watched the women smile.

The heavier woman let out a brief laugh, and Jack said, "This is Merlene." She smiled at Anthony and said, "And that's not *Mar*lene."

Merlene was warning Anthony of something. They began talking, exchanging the information of bars, who-do-you-knows in Westchester and Manhattan, though neither had many Manhattan contacts anymore.

Anthony watched Denise behind Merlene, her hands and arms; he followed her huge, squared-off fingernails in shining cherry red and her eyes with the blue paint underneath.

She was like the girl a few years ago, before Beth, who looked like Liza Minnelli, had that same joyous manic energy, and was wearing Frederic's underwear. But as he touched her the voice that came out of her was like tears, like grief: *please don't please don't please don't* over and over, something pathological in the poor girl, but it got inside him with its fear. And when he confided in Jack, the old Sarfatti dismissed her as one of the Catholic girls who dress like trollops and think like nuns.

Anthony moved to the right of Merlene as they all turned now to the bar. "Tell me what it is you do," she was saying.

"I manage part of a large corporation—an engineering section."

"Jack said you'd be too modest. That you're one of the big bosses."

"Well, let's say that right now my job lets me push Jack and the other engineers around. The rights of a boss is to *skootch* others."

She smiled at a familiar word and said, "You must be Italian, using that word."

"Doesn't everybody know that word by now?"

Merlene was smiling. "They don't even know we're not all in the Mafia—yet."

"I have a librarian friend, looks like a mouse—a mouse who's been beaten down—with the same name as a big gangster. They give him special tables soon as they hear the name in a restaurant or other places—"

"If they really wanted to catch crooks, let them catch the Colombians—killing people on the streets of Queens. They kill cops, they'd kill anything on the streets, and I mean senators, ministers. They sell nuclear bomb stuff that goes inside the bomb. They inject people with AIDS. They change people's brains."

Anthony reacted abruptly, and the woman noticed it. "Something go wrong?" she said. "Anything I said?"

"No, no, not at all. I just remembered I have to brief Jack before he flies out to Denver tomorrow. And I didn't bring my briefcase with my notes. Hey Jack!" He had leaned over the bar to get Jack's attention. "Let me run up and get my briefcase and we'll do a little briefing."

"Want me to walk with you?" Merlene said.

"No, I'll just jog it and be right back."

Her face showed that she was caught in the midst of response. Anthony left on that hesitation, catching Jack's uncomprehending eyes—he knew there was no need for the case.

Anthony did not know what to tell him—only that he had to get away. In the street he jogged and on the elevator heard his breathing like radio static. Once inside his apartment he double-locked the door and placed a kitchen chair against it. He did not know what he would say when the phone rang or if he would answer. But he knew he would not go back.

JOSEPH PAPALEO

Joe Papaleo has published stories and novels about Italian Americans for more than thirty-five years. "At first," *he says, "the stories were descriptive, like remembered portraits and pictures. Then they were little symbolic discoveries and epiphanies."*

Of late, he has been writing a new kind of ethnic story, where the assimilated ethnic is surprised by discovering the unchanged and rejected past within him and finds a new kind of alienation as his fate. The present story, "Friday Supper," is an example.

He has published two novels, All the Comforts *and* Out of Place, *the novella* Arete', *and short stories in* Commentary, The New Yorker, Harpers, Penthouse, Paris Review, *and many other magazines.*

Joe has been head of the writing department at Sarah Lawrence and is also an editor at Delphinium Books.

URBAN DESIGN

URBAN DESIGN

The Forms of Things Yet Unknown

Paul Rudolph

CIENCE MAY BE THE AUTHORITY, AND GOVERNMENT THE POWER, BUT both must help restore a humanness to our environment. Can a city, a neighborhood, or a university campus be a work of art in the twentieth century? Can—or should—our cities, with their constantly changing functional requirements, be turned into anything more than sociologically acceptable, characterless non-places? Is the city so complex that it is no longer possible to render it whole? Have the automobile and the sheer bulk of buildings, necessitated by the population explosion, made it impossible to create a human environment?

City planning—or urban design—is an art, and the most complex and important of all the arts. It is only through the courage of administrators, boards of trustees, governmental officials, and heads of industry that the current brutalization of "man-made America" can be rerouted.

The current energy crisis will help, not hinder, the humanization of our cities. Since Stonehenge, man has passionately striven to organize his environment, to create the ideal city, the ultimate and most enduring expression of any age. He still aspires, but there is growing confusion. Most planners today are lawyers.

Urban design, as opposed to the design of a single building, is concerned with the relationship of every element to every other element, so that the whole is greater than its parts. It is concerned with the relationship of buildings to each other, the form of the space between the buildings, of solids to voids, of buildings to the ground and to the sky, of internal spaces to the exterior form, of sculpture and painting to the building, and, most important in our century, the relationship of buildings to graphics and the paraphernalia embodying every means of transportation.

Today, architects are supposed to design buildings and lawyers do the planning for them. But buildings depend on their environment, both existing and future.

We think too much of the building as an entity within itself. The Parthenon depends on its setting atop the Acropolis, on the sequence of spaces revealed as one approaches, on its mysterious relationships to the mountains beyond, and on the eternal and incomparable clarity of the sunlight. All of these elements blend and interact so that finally the ensemble becomes the symbol for an age. It is difficult to imagine a group of lawyers planning the Acropolis, committees determining its needs and functions, economists calculating the budget for Mr. Elgin's marbles.

Our great twentieth-century architects had notions regarding urban design, but since they were revolutionaries, they tended to think that everything in sight must be torn down and a completely fresh start made.

Mr. Wright thought that no architect had ever lived before him and that probably no one would live after him. Therefore, it was not necessary for urban design to grow out of existing environment.

Le Corbusier thought that Paris should be torn down and that his own buildings, in a park, should replace them. Fortunately, this did not happen.

Gropius prepared elaborate graphs, plotting the course of the sun, and suggested a pseudoscientific approach to the placement of buildings, complete with statistics, graphs, and precomputer data.

Mies was content with placing his beautiful packages on whatever site his client happened to own.

Contrary to popular opinion, the creative process is, ultimately, highly impersonal. The urban designer-architect, -painter, and -sculptor must direct his inner vision towards those problems and opportunities of an age and drive towards those essences which differentiate one epoch from another in order to render it simultaneously timeless and of its time. Any artist is merely an instrument who senses the drives of an age and helps translate them into an environment which serves man.

Any work of art, if it is to rise above the immediate, must recognize the forces at play in society. The artist has little to do with these forces, but if his inner vision is accurately focused on the needs, the aspirations, the desires (some more admirable than others) of an epoch, then his work will rise above the merely pretty, the sentimental, the provincial, the expedient, and ultimately be seen as speaking in its own unique and peculiar way for an age.

Herbert Read puts it this way:

> I do not believe that the masses can have a culture of
> their own, distinct from the culture of the aristocrat:

at least, such a culture, like peasant art, would be of minor interest. But the masses are necessary to a culture as soil is necessary to a flower: and there is no culture unless an intimate relationship, at the level of instinct, exists between a people and its poets. One cannot repeat too often, because it is the distinctive characteristic of any humanism, that the images of wholeness that the poet creates out of his own inner contradictions are at the same time symbols of reconciliation for the conflict of instinct and spirit in a people. Without this intimate correspondence, art remains esoteric and the people remain barbaric.

Modern art, it will be said, is and will remain esoteric. I think it is presumptuous to make such an assertion. For a long time Greek art of the Archaic period was esoteric, a tribal art or a magical art, but gradually became the art of a civilization. For a long time the art of the catacombs remained esoteric, until it blossomed into the art of byzantium and the western world. Even the art of the Renaissance began as an esoteric cult of antiquity.

Artists are essential to a civilization but do not create it.

What is an architect's contribution to his environment? The urban designer-architect is impotent unless he recognizes the forces in society and translates these forces or desires into three-dimensional reality. What are the twentieth-century forces that must be tamed, understood, deflected? They are: (1) materialism; (2) the population explosion, necessitating a sheer increase in size; and (3) the impact of science on our society.

The prime force in our country is the materialistic one, aggravated by an increasing and mobile population and the consequently changing political and economic configurations. Materialism has a love affair with first costs which, in turn, are usually less, if precedents are followed, which, in turn, unduly penalizes the creative.

The strictly materialistic approach is unspirited, deadening, and brutalizes all too often the original that it emulated. But Venice was an almost completely materialistic economy, and look what it did. The building as advertisement is, I believe, as valid as, say, St. Peter's, which stands for the power of the Catholic Church. The danger with a building that is a special type of advertisement is that it ignores its antecedents, overstates its case, and doesn't respect the larger context in which it is placed.

Our commitment to individualism is partially a reaction to the growing conformity of the twentieth century, but more important it is caused by the excitement of sensing magnificent new forces and their possibilities. There are too many new worlds to explore, too many problems crying for solutions for there to be a universal outlook.

The second force, sheer bulk, has caused provision for communications to become the dominant element in our physical environment. Road Town USA and the highways are the result. The American genius for building thruways, bridges, intersections—rendering them as voluptuous as a Rubens painting—is deep in the American tradition of going on, on, on. There is an assuredness of form when dealing with the *moving* automobile that is often breathtaking. It is noteworthy that we seldom question the amount of money spent to get our cars from one place to another. However, the machine when at rest seldom seems happy, warring with its surroundings, indignant at being relegated to a slum of asphalt, ungainly lighting standards, multitudinous signs begetting other signs. The automobile, accustomed to the splendors of the open road, is usually sad in its minimum car park, and its occupant often has difficulty getting from car to building. In turn, many buildings are almost entirely swallowed by the armadas of cars threatening them.

Most airports are fine examples of environmental possibilities. The juncture of dissimilar forms, or the joint, is a prime detriment of all form and so it is between car and building. Kennedy Airport is confused and confusing because it is fundamentally an interchange but it reads like a huge parking lot (and in the middle are stuck three religious buildings, which don't have a chance). The buildings are fundamentally an advertisement for the airlines involved. However, an airport is, finally, a gateway and, for many, a gateway to this country. All its parts should add up to one memorable moment instead of being the architectural zoo that it is.

But great urban design is often the result of remodeling. Witness Michelangelo's Campidoglio in Rome, where he transformed a medieval mess into a great work of art. It was easier then because the car did not exist. The car is the problem, but inherent in the problems of form are elements so large that they can be used to organize much of the urban scene.

Yes, transportation systems and their relationship to the building will become the chief characteristic of the middle twentieth-century city. Le Corbusier foresaw all of this in his proposals for Algiers and the raised roadbed, which becomes a building or series of buildings several miles long.

The proposed lower Manhattan expressway is usually discussed in terms of being above the ground (at about half the cost) or below the ground. But it would be a different story if the raised expressway were conceived as a building or series of buildings with the roadbed at the top. Such a building, two or three miles long, should adapt itself to the existing buildings on either side. The "no-man's-land" between expressway and the existing cityscape can become the open space between buildings, and therefore a connection rather than a means of separating buildings from cars.

The automobile is, in a sense, an outer garment which needs to be stored in a closet from time to time. Lewis Mumford called it "the insolent monster," and it is true that it takes on rather human characteristics from time to time. However, it is something to be tamed and humanized, not made fun of. Our filling stations are the modern equivalent of the village well.

The increased needs of communications have resulted in often beautiful sentinels and supports for radar and other electronic paraphernalia, which is a new kind of sculpture. Is it possible that signs and billboards are the most valid form of adornment of the exterior environment for the twentieth century? Mrs. Lyndon Johnson's war on billboards, in their usual form and placement, was admirable. But this does not negate the fact that in sophisticated hands there is more color, verve, and spirit inherent in twentieth-century graphic art than in most easel painting. It is not integrated into the fabric of our environment partially because we look down on graphic art. The Renaissance would have known what to do with neon tubing. Certainly, the stained-glass artists of Chartres Cathedral would have reveled in it. If the colorist who painted out the Parthenon's marbles had had our factory finishes, he would surely have been elated.

Our pop artists have helped show the connections between graphic art and urban design. Times Square should have five times as many neon signs to completely hide all those ugly buildings, but its next door "room," the New York Public Library Plaza, should have none.

The third prime force, the contribution of science to our environment, makes it possible to make even higher, safer, quieter, more comfortable buildings. Science has given this country so many different choices of building materials and structural systems that it is often bewildering. Of course, the machine can imitate nature and create antiques by machine, with wood and marble finishes stamped on machine-made finishes (they are often preferred to the real thing, although they are obviously a falsehood). The machine-made finish often seems unhuman, partially because it does not wear and consequently change with human use. Mies and Gropius evolved an architecture that looked as if it had been made by machine, although it was at first an architecture dependent on superior craftsmanship.

The high point of the machine aesthetic was possibly reached in Manhattan's Seagram Building, paradoxically finished in bronze and travertine, timeless building materials. The machine aesthetic, in strictly architectural terms, has come to mean buildings whose form is fundamentally a box package, where all signs of life or human activity are hidden behind endlessly repeated glass or lightweight panels of absolute regularity, as if the machine was limited to producing regular panels. By the strength of his proportions and precision of detailing, Mies raised this formula to a high art indeed. But two factors inherent in this demanding concept of architecture have rendered it impotent. The first, and most important, is the fact that it is difficult to develop a sense of "place" with elephantine packages whose size and placement are determined by real estate interests, and situated according to arbitrary ownership of parcels of land. We are currently witnessing the rise and fall of the curtain wall. It has been shown conclusively that the curtain wall can only be refined, not used to make a "place" for our rushing crowds to rush to, a definitive prerequisite for an age which is manufacturing people at such a rapid rate. Second, packages don't lend themselves to an appropriate hierarchy of building types. They depend mostly on size and materials for their effect. More important, they cannot be readily joined, forming "walls" to define "rooms" and different environments for the city.

Quickly, everyone grows tired of the package (even though they tend to be the cheapest). And so the structural system and infilling skin has been decorated in various ways by many architects.

The principal alternate to package architecture grows out of Frank Lloyd Wright's and Le Corbusier's concepts that man's spirit and infinite modes of expression need to be made manifest, celebrated, and encouraged. Architecturally, this means that the various kinds of buildings need to be made explicit: thus, a school would never resemble a factory; a multistoried apartment block would be clearly not an office tower—which is what Mies thinks. A southern town would have a different character from a northern one, and the whole would grow and change.

In so many ways flexibility, the enemy of architecture, would be limited as much as possible, since it tends to become characterless. Those elements which are truly fixed, like elevators, stairs, stacks of toilets, structural and mechanical systems, would be emphasized, and special rooms would be made manifest, accentuated, differentiated, and made into anchors for the more mundane functions in the building.

Such buildings are never complete within themselves but are thought of as a point in time, always growing and changing. *Change is the only constant in the twentieth century.* Urban design must be relearned, recognizing again that a city can be a work of art but that the artist must direct his inner vision towards the problems which society, not he, poses. The forces of society are materialism, the tremendous bulk and communication problems caused by the population explosion, and the impact of science. Only through art can we remain human.

In *A Midsummer Night's Dream* you will find this: "And as imagination bodies forth the forms of things unknown, the poet's pen turns them to shapes, and gives to airy nothing a local habitation and a name."

Urban design is remodeling, adding, subtracting, reworking, relating, and reforming three-dimensional spaces for human activities, including all pedestrian and vehicular systems. Urban design deals with the old and the new, the expanded and the contracted, the humdrum and the extraordinary. It brings people together. It separates people. It commemorates its history. It never lies but portrays life three-dimensionally, as it really is. At its best, it creates related and usable exterior spaces, provides means of getting "there," and a "there" once you are "there." It is the mother art of civilization, for it allows, and indeed demands, ideas, thinking, reactions to opportunities of the moment, executed in the spirit of its time, and demands respect for its earlier efforts. The new depends upon the old and is responsible for the future. If the old is ignored, misunderstood, the future will mock the seemingly new and reveal for all to

plainly see the false thinking expressed. All the other arts
are handmaidens to urban design.

P A U L   R U D O L P H

*He is one of our precious architectural visionaries. In this
essay he pleads for cities with a sense of their proper
harmonies. In doing this, he increases our awareness of
shapes and spaces in a new way. For example, he dis-
cusses ways to make the automobile and the building fit
side by side in urban structures. He shows how the art of
urban design demands the talents of artist, architect,
and planner.*

*"Urban Design" speaks with a deceptively simple
voice as it creates a complex and as yet unrealized sche-
matic of a proper future city. We are ever so grateful to
him for opening our eyes to another solution for solving
the problems of our complex environment.*

AUTUMN

AUTUMN

Anitra Peebles Sheen

EVERY DAY HE WALKED ALONG THE GARDEN PATH THAT SUR-rounded the rectory, the tops of his shoes pushing forward under the long black cassock. As he walked, he held open his breviary with both hands, often shaping the words with his mouth as he read the Divine Office. I walked up the corridor between the church and the school and saw him pacing slowly, his breviary open. But he wasn't reading; he was looking sideways over the schoolyard.

When I approached the garden, he lowered his eyes and began mumbling the words, turning to a section of path bordered by white chrysanthemums and a low brick wall.

"Good afternoon, Father," I said nonchalantly, almost passing him.

"Hello, Annie," he said. "Cold today . . ."

"Yes, Father."

"Ready for Thanksgiving?"

"Not yet, Father," I said, as we started to walk along, side by side.

"Will you be cooking the turkey dinner by yourself?" he asked. He was interested in our life at home, and I sometimes caught him looking at me tentatively, as if I were a strange plant.

"Yes, Father. It's not hard; you just follow the directions in a cookbook."

"I'm sure it will be fine," he said, "better than fine."

"No one complains. Well, my brothers make faces occasionally, but they always eat." Father Marconi smiled his small smile. I smiled mine. This was that certain point in every conversation, the point at which we either passed on with a wave or entered into our subject: my crisis in faith.

Sister Margaret Mary, alarmed by my comments on our religion test, had suggested that I speak with Father Marconi—"take counsel with him" is what she said. Then she explained in a suitably awestruck voice that Jesuits were "broadly educated," so Father could answer all my questions. That was in September. Since then, we had talked often, but my faith was still on shaky ground.

The reason was not as Sister Margaret Mary thought, that mine was a new faith with shallow roots not yet able to hold fast in the depths of my soul. The reason was that mine was a chosen faith, and I took it seriously. I had converted from none to Catholic about a year before this crisis began, which was shortly before my thirteenth birthday. And although I had not become a crusader, I had become a secret fanatic. I had no tolerance for classmates who whispered and giggled during Mass, or sneaked cookies during the three-hour fast before Communion. How could they knowingly offend God? They didn't believe as I believed. During the year I studied the Church's teachings, I sucked them into my heart, and my every deed was guided by them. It was not my deeds, however, that had begun to trouble me, it was my thoughts. Now, I was relieved to be thirteen, having lied to Father Marconi because I couldn't admit to being twelve. At thirteen I had a right to serious doubts.

Our school uniform was a royal blue jumper with a white, short-sleeved blouse underneath. I liked wearing a uniform. It was easy to take care of, and it saved me the difficulty of acquiring clothes. As we had no mother and a father who was oblivious to such matters, our clothes situation was always catch-as-catch-can. This never seemed to bother my brothers, but it was obvious to me that the three of us were outside the realm of whatever it was that enabled other kids to appear in proper order. But in my uniform, I was as neat and correct as any other girl. Only my soul was in disarray.

"Father, I understand about Sanctifying Grace, but I don't think I can accept it."

"What exactly can't you accept?"

"That only those people with Sanctifying Grace at the moment of death will be saved. What about the person who lives a good life, but commits a mortal sin just before he gets killed in an accident? It's not fair that he's sentenced to hell forever."

Father Marconi closed his book and sighed. He was used to my questions, but he didn't give ready answers. He was careful; he took his time.

As I waited for his answer, the brick wall felt cold and hard beneath me, and I shifted my weight, uncrossing and recrossing my legs. Father Marconi stood close and motionless.

"God is merciful," he said.

Although Father Marconi was in his early forties, his

hair showed not a trace of grey. It was black and wavy like Persian lamb. His hands were large, long-fingered, and beautiful, with a scattering of dark hair that grew dense and disappeared under the cuff of his sleeve. I had watched these hands lift the Host during Mass, anoint foreheads, making the sign of the cross with his thumb. I had watched them turn gold-edged pages and write with bold strokes on the blackboard: *Agnus Dei* . . . Lamb of God, *qui tollis peccata mundi* . . . who takest away the sins of the world, *Miserere nobis* . . . Have mercy on us.

Recently I had found myself thinking about Father Marconi's hands, how beautiful they were, how strong they would be, how gentle. I would think of his hands outstretched during High Mass, the censer swinging like a pendulum from his fingers, the sweet smell of incense wafting up from his arms, his vestments gleaming with gold embroidery. I imagined his hands in candlelight, unbuttoning his white embroidered cuffs.

The next time I saw him he was standing beside the maple tree that had begun to shed its red-orange leaves on the rectory lawn. He stood in the warm afternoon light, a black silhouette; he was smiling. "And they say that southern California doesn't have seasons! Just look at this," he said, laughing, dropping a bunch of crackling leaves into my hands. I was surprised by his lightness of mood and didn't quite know how to respond. The tone of our conversations had always been formal: teacher to student, adult to child, unequal. There was something comfortable in this and safe. "I guess we all welcome a change of season," he said, his face growing serious.

"Yes, Father," I said, letting some leaves fall from my hands.

"And what were you wondering about today, Annie?" He was serious now, and somehow powerful in his black robes, powerful and wise.

"Well," I said, "at home we've been reading about the Van Allen belts. You know, the bands of radiation that surround the earth."

"Yes, I know," he said.

"Well, the Church says that the Virgin Mary was assumed into heaven, body and soul. How could she, without burning up? My father says it's impossible."

"Is that what he said?"

"Well, not exactly. What he said was, 'She'd singe her tail feathers.' "

"Well, well," he said, laughing. "That sounds like him. . . . You know, I met your father a few nights ago. A family had called me in to give the last rites to an old patient of his. Big family. Seems he takes care of them all."

"Did you talk to him?"

"Briefly. I don't think he liked me very much; he knows I'm your religion teacher. What puzzles me is why he allowed you to convert. He obviously doesn't believe in the Church. Why didn't he try to stop you . . . or did he?"

"No, he just said it was my decision."

"That's all?"

"And that I'd grow out of it."

"You think that is what's happening now, Annie?" He placed his hand lightly on top of my head, as if checking my height. "You are growing," he said. "I've watched you. . . ." I knew he watched me. I had known it for a long time.

"I want to believe, Father," I said. "It's just that I have questions." It was true. I did want to believe. I wanted all the truths intact. I wanted the certainty of Truth. I felt if I could be certain of what sin was, I would not sin. If I knew for certain what I should do, I would do it. These growing doubts gave me a freedom I didn't want; I had already had too much of it and knew its burden.

On the Wednesday before Thanksgiving I made a list, because I knew if I forgot something, I'd be sunk. Turkey, potatoes, onions, celery, cranberry sauce, canned peas, pumpkin pie. I had already gotten the bread from the Helm's truck, butter and whipping cream from the milk-man. With the crisp twenty-dollar bills my father had given me, I walked the two miles to the market, then took a taxi back, loaded with groceries. I gave all the change I had left to the taxi driver. It wasn't much.

When I got home, the house was dark and empty. I turned on the lights and put on a record: Vivaldi's "Four Seasons," mood music for Thanksgiving. I was used to spending afternoons and evenings alone now. My father's days were increasingly long, and my brothers, deep into teenage, had begun slipping away into secret lives of their own. Jimmy came home first, usually after dinnertime. Alex came home late, sometimes not at all. We closed our eyes to Alex and opened them only when he would act normal. Normal is what we required.

When our family was together, usually on Sundays, we were careful to stay on common ground. This ground, its designation never acknowledged but understood, was sacred and essential. It had no seasons. We talked about science and current events. My father talked about his patients, some of whom we had known all our lives. What we didn't talk about was my faith (or crisis thereof), that I had chosen Catholic school, or that Alex had chosen to drop out. We didn't talk about the fact that Alex no longer played the piano, except on the rare occasions when we could coax him to play pieces for four hands. We didn't talk about the times we found my father short of breath or stopping on the stairs, rubbing his shoulder, his lips dusky and wincing. "Pulled a muscle," he would say if we approached him. I believed him; it's what I wanted him to say.

I understood this only years later, when I remembered a story my father told me. A patient had called him to make a house call to see her ill husband. She said her husband had vomited blood and was resting on the floor. When my father arrived, he saw that the man had blown his brains out; the gun was still lying beside him.

"Didn't she see what happened?" I asked.

"No," said my father. "She couldn't see it . . . at least, not at that moment."

On Thursday evening, we sat at the table, playing out our normal Thanksgiving dinner. The table was decorated with red and gold leaves that I had picked up along the street. In the center of the table was a branch of pyracantha, laden with brilliant berries and crawling with little bugs because I hadn't thought to wash it off. "Allow me, Senorita, on thees especial occasion," Jimmy said as he pulled out my chair. Only, as I started to sit, he pulled it out farther and watched with surprise when I slowly sunk to the floor, without losing my balance.

"Good trick, Annie," said Alex. It was good to see him smile.

Everything was normal: Pass the mashed potatoes. More turkey? Light or dark? My father did not slip a pill under his tongue. Alex did not smell of alcohol. Jimmy did not make desperate jokes, one after the other. I cut the pumpkin pie into large wedges, topping them with overly whipped cream, almost butter. My father watched me as if I were a stranger, as if sizing me up. When he decided the moment was right, he looked at me and said, "I met Friar

Macaroni." (This was a good sign. Teasing about a name is normal.)

"I know; he told me," I said.

"Did he tell you that I kicked him out of the room?"

"You did?"

"I had to. He almost scared poor ol' William to death. There I was trying to give William some encouragement, when Macaroni walks in, slaps down this big cross on the bed, then opens up his black kit. I wasn't sure what it meant, but ol' William's eyes almost popped out of his head. And then he started gasping for breath. . . . So, I kicked him out."

"And how's ol' William now?"

My father looked up from his pie. "Alive," he said.

Jimmy looked at my father, then at me. He had that canny look about him, his dimples all pulled in, his eyes squeezed into little mounds. "So, Annie's got a crush on Friar Macaroni!" he said.

"Don't be ridiculous!"

"Then how come your face pops open when you hear his name?"

"It does not. And his name is Marconi, you know, like the inventor of the wireless . . ."

"You have a crush on the inventor of the wireless?"

"I do not. And that's a terrible thing to say; he's a priest."

Putting down his fork, my father looked at me from under his bushy eyebrows. It was his Pay-attention-I'm-only-going-to-say-it-once look.

"A priest is a man, Annie," he said. "Standard issue."

A week after Thanksgiving, it was record-breaking hot.

Camellia buds failed to open and fell to the ground, brown as snails. Polar bear signs were hung outside the movie theaters—"Air cooled" they said. The girls at school opened the top button of their uniform blouses. I opened two.

After school, Father Marconi and I walked along the side path where it was shady. Even in his black gabardine cassock, he always appeared cool. But on this day he pulled at his white collar and shook his shoulders now and then, as if his clothes were sticking to him.

"Father, do you really think Limbo is a place?" I asked.

"It could be a place, if you take the Scripture literally," he said. His eyes were heavy on my chest, on the empty button holes. "Or," he continued in a halting voice, "it could be something like a state of mind, a plane of existence."

It was hard to reconcile what I had envisioned as a horde of empty-eyed souls, straining toward heaven, with a "plane of existence." It was too hot to grasp anything so obscure. I focused instead on several chrysanthemums, weakened from the heat, that had fallen over and were lying face down on the path. I bent down to pick them up. I knew that Father Marconi was standing over me, looking. I knew that he would before I bent down.

"Sister Margaret Mary says that the unbaptized go there . . . to Limbo," I said. "They just park there until the Judgment Day."

Slowly, he reached over and softly slid the back of his hand down my neck, then buttoned my blouse starting from the top, his fingers pressing lightly against my skin. I looked straight ahead, facing the black covered chest and the chain with Christ on the cross.

The words came fast and breathless: "That means all

the people who lived before Christ and most of the people who lived after him can't be with God. They just stay suspended."

"Annie, why are you so concerned about Limbo?" he said, turning away.

"Alex and Jimmy aren't baptized and they don't want to be. Most of the people in the world aren't Christian. How can God reject them?"

For a long time we walked in silence, doubling back toward the shade when the sun beat from the west into our eyes. The only sound was the soft whoosh of his cassock. I loved the rhythm of it, a cadence of unearthly music. Several times he took a deep breath as if to say something, stopped, then continued on in silence. Our shadows grew long on the sidewalk. "I should go home, Father," I said.

"Yes," he said. "We can talk about this tomorrow."

I reminded him that we would have only a half day of school, because the nuns would be attending the funeral of their Mother General.

"I know," he said, sucking in another breath, letting it out. "I could come to your house in the afternoon, and we could talk." After a few steps, he stopped abruptly and pulled me to the side of the path. His eyes were more intense than I had ever seen them.

"You understand what I'm saying?"

"Yes."

"And you want me to come?"

"Yes."

. . .

The next day was still hot, and it seemed the brief pause that was autumn had slipped by, leaving barely a mark in the year's cycle. The city smouldered under a layer of haze, making the Santa Clauses and giant snowflakes along Hollywood Boulevard seem incongruous and a lie. But the passage of days is relentless, even in Los Angeles, and we knew that winter was upon us, regardless of the temperature. To me, the problem of the heat was immediate; I would have to run all the way home after school let out, and I didn't want to be late.

At one o'clock the doorbell rang. I was shaky from running the three miles home, or perhaps it was something else. With my hair still dripping from the shower, I ran down the stairs, pulling on a shirt and pants as I went. "Hi," he said simply, as I opened the door.

"Hello," I replied, barely able to get the word out, barely able to believe my eyes. This was all wrong! He wasn't wearing his black clothes, but stood in blue-and-orange plaid slacks and a V-neck shirt with one pearlized button and one loop; it was not tucked in. The shoes he wore were brown and white with tassels, golfing shoes. In his hand, a little bunch of marguerites shyly wilted.

"Come in, Father," I said with a voice quivering more from shock than fear. It was not so much his clothes that shocked me; it was that he looked so ordinary. Here was a man you wouldn't look at twice on the street. He looked fatter and older, shorter and less substantial than the man I walked with just the day before. This was not the person I had expected. That man belonged with candlelight and the smell of beeswax, with his mystery cloaked in black cloth.

Sinking in dread and panic I led him into the living room and offered him a soft drink. "Not now," he said. He smiled his small smile; I smiled mine.

"You remember my question from yesterday, Father?" I asked lamely.

"Something about Limbo and baptism," he answered, his voice patient. "Do you want to talk about it?"

Yes I wanted to talk about it! I wanted to talk about anything—the weather, Christmas card sales, the miracle at Lourdes—anything that would stall for time and let me escape.

"We don't have to interpret Scripture literally," he said, running his cold hand along my cheek. "Scholars disagree on the interpretation of the Gospels." I looked down at the tassels on his shoes, fighting back a nervous urge to laugh.

What we saw at one-fifteen was not a vision. Jimmy came through the front door, and when he saw us sitting there his jaw dropped straight down.

"What are *you* doing home!" he said.

"What are *you* doing home!" I answered, leaping to my feet. "I have the afternoon off." Jimmy looked behind me. "Oh," I said without looking back; I could picture his face. "This is Father Marconi. Father, this is my brother Jimmy."

Jimmy's eyes fell on the blazing plaid slacks. "Hi," he said, staring shamelessly. Only then did I notice a small figure eclipsed behind Jimmy's back. Slowly she slid out from behind him, wide-eyed as a cornered cat. Her hair was in a "bubble," held back with a thin pink ribbon tied in the middle. One loop of the bow had come undone, and she was making little puffs with her lower lip, trying to blow it off her forehead. "Father?" she said in a tiny voice. Trying to be matter-of-fact, but giving himself away with too many uhs and ums, Jimmy explained that I was his sister and that Father Marconi was my religion teacher.

"Oooh," she said.

"We can talk another time, Annie," said Father Marconi as he walked toward the front door. His face was pale and his lips were drawn in as if he were chewing on them. I walked with him to the door and paused a moment before opening it. For the first time I saw him plainly—Joseph Marconi—someone with his own questions and his own doubts. His pain struck me low in the stomach. This was not just an embarrassment for him. He had come to the brink of a felony and worse, a mortal sin. Yet, I knew it was also my sin. I had brought him to the edge and said yes.

That night there was a cold front from the north and winds from the ocean swept over the city. We opened our windows to the crisp night air. Autumn had returned, unexpected. Jimmy didn't mention the incident again, nor did I. It merely seeped into the groundwater of things unspoken. But we had learned something about each other, not only that we were growing up, but also that each of us was capable of a secret life that excluded the other.

For a while, Jimmy came home earlier. And we hiked in the hills behind our house and gathered pine cones sticky with resin. We went to see the reindeer in a corral on Wilshire Boulevard. That time together was reassuring and enough. Soon Jimmy returned to his other weekday life. "See you Sunday, old girl," he said.

"Okay," I said. "Gather ye rosebuds while ye may . . ."

"Herrick," he said. "Now it is autumn and the falling fruit . . ." Jimmy was standing now, his hand on his chest, projecting his voice. ". . . and the long journey towards oblivion . . ."

"Lawrence," I said. "Too dramatic. . . . Not oblivion, good brother, if you take the 'Road to Mandalay.' Come you back to Mandalay . . ."

"Kipling," said Jimmy. "Mandalay! That's the place

where memories stay . . ."

"Who said that?"

"Me."

At three o'clock school let out. Disorderly lines of children spilled from the doors, a flood of little heads swirling in blue and white. Father Marconi stood close to the door and stepped out when he saw me. "I want to talk to you," he said. "Come walk with me." It was the first time we had spoken since that day at our house. Whether he had looked for me I didn't know, since I had been leaving right after school, trying to avoid him. But this meeting was not as awkward as I expected, and I followed him to the rectory path quite at ease. The ground was bare along the flower borders for the chrysanthemums had been cut to the ground, and nothing had been planted to replace them. As we walked around to the back of the garden, I listened to the whoosh of his robe. Its rhythm was familiar and pleasant, as was his warmth beside me. Boldly, he took my hand in his. "I'm going away," he said.

"Where?"

"To a mission school we have in New Mexico. I asked to be transferred there."

I asked him when he would be leaving. "Soon," he said, "the end of December." I walked ahead of him for a while, trying to imagine his absence. At the gate, he held out his hand to say goodbye. It was an ordinary hand, a man's hand.

ANITRA PEEBLES SHEEN

Our questions on the story "Autumn" got Anitra Sheen talking about themes, those ideas that stay with writers longer than story ideas and are often the background of several stories.

Later, she wrote: " 'Autumn,' its situation and events, is part of a larger story about a motherless family. However, this particular story did not begin with its events, but rather with two different ideas, one relating to form and the other relating to theme.

"I thought it would be interesting to write a story in which the dialogue between the main characters is about one thing while the subtext of the story is about something else. I wanted to keep the two levels very clear, but separate.

"I had been thinking about Nabokov's Lolita, *about the complicity of children and the extent of a child's capacity for moral choice. With these two seeds in hand, I returned to the development of this family, to see where I could plant them."*

Anitra Sheen is a medical writer who is based in Los Angeles. This is her first published fiction.